Chasing Happiness, Not Chaos

Tonya McBean, MS

Brookscraft Publishing

Chasing Happiness, Not Chaos

Published 2026 by:
Brookscraft Publishing
Buffalo, New York 14203
info@brookscraftpublishing.com
https://brookscraftpublishing.com

ISBN Paperback: 978-1-969682-53-7

Title: Chasing Happiness, Not Chaos
Author: Tonya McBean, MS
Copyright: © 2026 Tonya McBean, MS

Printed and bound in the United States of America

Dedication

To every person carrying more than they show, doing more than being thanked for, and loving more than they receive. May you stop chasing chaos and find happiness again—not in perfection or performance, but in the God who knows your name, sees your heart, and holds your peace.

— Tonya McBean

Table of Contents

Foreword

We live in a world that tells us happiness is something we have to earn. That we'll feel fulfilled "one day," after we've worked harder, waited longer, proven ourselves more, or finally found the missing puzzle piece- the job, the partner, the money, the look, the moment. But real happiness doesn't wait on permission.

Joy is not something that happens to us—it's something we learn to create from the inside out. And as life gets louder, faster, and more demanding, often the first thing we lose sight of is ourselves. We get swept up in chaos—in busy schedules, overflowing responsibilities, and expectations that stretch us beyond our limits.

This book is an invitation to come home. To your breath. To your peace. To your inner voice that whispers, **"There has to be another way."**

Inside these pages, you'll explore what it truly means to build happiness from the ground up—in your thoughts, in your habits, in your boundaries, and in your heart.

You'll learn when to hold on and when to let go. When to speak up and when to walk away. When to rest, and when to rise. You'll see that **joy isn't naïve**—it's powerful. **Peace isn't passive**—it's intentional. And **calm isn't found by chance**—it's created by choice.

Because when you stop chasing chaos, you realize happiness was never hiding. It was waiting, patiently, for you to notice it.

Welcome to the beginning of your next chapter. Welcome to a life built on purpose, presence, and peace.

Introduction

Most of us don't realize how tired we are until we slow down long enough to feel it. We wake up already behind. We move through the day on autopilot, too busy to care as we drift from one task to the next. We measure our worth by what we accomplish, who we please, and how well we hold everything together. Checking things off the list becomes the norm. We forget what we really want because life gets in the way. And somewhere between trying to stay strong, be available, keep up, and take care of everyone else, we quietly lose track of ourselves.

We trade peace for pressure. Joy for obligation. Rest for performance. Presence for productivity.

We end up chasing happiness, believing it lives just beyond where we are.

"If I can just get through this season. . ."

"If life would slow down. . ."

"If I could fix this one thing. . ."

"If they could finally understand. . ."

But happiness that has to be chased is happiness that always runs away. This book is your invitation to stop running. Stop chasing. Stop striving.

A Different Kind of Journey

True happiness isn't waiting on the other side of a perfect week, a better relationship, a cleaner house, a quieter schedule, or a life where nothing goes wrong. True happiness is built from the inside out—from peace, boundaries, gratitude, faith, and the courage to choose joy on purpose.

This book is not about changing your circumstances but about changing the way you experience them. In the chapters that follow, you'll learn how to:

- Let go of what drains you

- Slow down without guilt

- Protect your energy and your heart

- Stop overthinking your way out of peace

- Find rest right where you are

- Seek meaning instead of noise

- Choose joy in imperfect days

Life will improve not because it suddenly becomes easy but because you anchor differently inside it.

You Don't Have to Earn Joy

You weren't created to live exhausted, anxious, or emotionally thin. You were made for:

- Stillness

- Wonder

- Gratitude

- Laughter

- Connection

- Purpose

- Quiet confidence

God did not design you to outrun your life. He designed you to live it and find contentment. You were made for a life that feels like it fits your soul.

A Gentle Reminder

You are not behind. You are not too late. You have not missed your moment. You do not need to prove yourself worthy of rest or happiness. If you desire peace, if your heart aches for something steadier, or if you are tired of chaos making decisions for you, you are already standing at the doorway.

All that's left is to step through.

What You'll Discover Here

This book will help you:

- Untangle hurry

- Clear space for what matters

- Build boundaries that protect your joy

- Recognize the small daily choices that add up to peace

- Return to the God who fills the places nothing else can reach

You'll move from striving to surrender, from chaos to clarity, from hurrying to stillness. Instead of searching, you'll feel steady and satisfied right where you are. Happiness stops being a finish line and becomes a way of living.

One Step at a Time

You don't have to change everything today. You don't have to master every chapter. You don't have to have it all figured out.

All you have to do is start: one breath, one step, one small shift at a time. If you are ready, I'll walk with you, chapter by chapter, out of the noise and into the calm that has been calling you back home.

Welcome to *Chasing Happiness, Not Chaos.*

Part I:
TURNING INWARD

Chapter 1:

Happiness Is an Inside Job

Happiness is one of the most misunderstood pursuits on the planet. We chase it like something we have to catch—a runaway balloon floating just out of reach. We're raised to believe that happiness is a reward we earn if we achieve, impress, or endure enough.

We tell ourselves that we'll be happy once we get married, get a house, or have a baby. That happiness will arrive once we're more successful or once we fix everything that feels broken.

But this is a myth. If happiness depends on circumstances being just right, we will live our lives waiting instead of living.

Happiness Begins Within

Real happiness starts inside you: in your mind, your beliefs, your values, and in the way you speak to and honor yourself.

When you build happiness internally, storms don't break you. Disappointments don't define you. Chaos loses its power. In short, you become anchored instead of blown around by life.

Happiness begins within and is supported by decades of scientific research. It's not just a man-made mantra. It is proven that happiness depends on how the brain interprets events, regulates emotions, and forms meaning, rather than by external circumstances alone.

The Brain Responds to Interpretation, Not Events

Neuroscience shows that events themselves have no power to create happiness or unhappiness, but the way we interpret those events does.

- The brain's emotional centers respond to how we perceive a situation.

- Two people can experience the same situation and feel completely different emotions based on their internal beliefs, expectations, and self-talk.

- Happiness is shaped internally by meaning-making, not externally by circumstances.

Why We Look Outside Ourselves

External happiness is appealing because it's quick. It can take the form of new clothes, entertainment, busyness, praise, and achievements. These feel good temporarily, but the effect fades, and we're soon back searching for the next hit.

External happiness is sugar—fast and fleeting. Internal happiness is nourishment—lasting and stabilizing.

Modern research on social media and validation shows:

- Social comparisons activate dopamine briefly.

- The brain quickly craves more validation.

- Being dependent on external validation increases anxiety and self-doubt.

- In contrast:

- Internal validation builds up more stable emotional circuits.

- Self-acceptance enhances independence rather than comparison.

- Happiness that depends on others is temporary; happiness rooted within has a long-term effect.

Inner Joy Is a Skill

Building internal joy requires intention. It calls for slowing down, being present, and listening inward. It requires getting honest about your needs and challenging beliefs that no longer serve you.

The work is quieter, but cultivating inner happiness creates a life that feels grounded and real.

Happiness depends heavily on how we regulate our emotions, which needs to be learned and practiced internally.

Research shows that people who report higher well-being tend to:

♦ Reflect before reacting.

♦ Accept emotions rather than ignoring them.

♦ Choose responses logically.

These are internal skills, not externally given circumstances.

Happiness begins when a person feels emotionally safe within their skin.

Three Pillars of Inner Happiness

1. Self-Compassion

Speak to yourself like someone you love. Replace criticism with curiosity. And stop punishing yourself for being human. We don't control life events, but we do control how our mind, heart, and spirit meet those events.

2. Self-Trust

When you trust yourself, you stop second-guessing. You release the pressure to be perfect, and you no longer outsource joy based on other people's approval. By this, we create more lasting happiness than pleasure.

3. Self-Truth

Know who you are. Ask yourself, **"What are my values, strengths, needs, and priorities?"** Joy cannot grow in a life built on someone else's expectations. External pleasure is short-lived because it is adapted.

The World Rewards Chaos

Today's hustle culture glorifies constant availability, instant gratification, and busyness over well-being. That means that slowing down, protecting your soul, and choosing stillness can feel rebellious. But reclaiming your peace is the bravest rebellion of all. Your mind processes everything you expose it to. News cycles, social media, conversations, and constant notifications overstimulate the nervous system, keeping the brain in a state of alert.

Practical steps:

◆ Limit news intake to particular times.

◆ Unfollow accounts and people that provoke anxiety, comparison, or outrage.

◆ Silence notifications that are not needed.

The Shift That Changes Everything

When you understand happiness begins inside, you stop trying to fix everyone else. You stop waiting for "perfect," which is a myth. You give yourself permission to be enough. And in doing these things, life feels lighter—even when circumstances don't change. Protecting peace does not mean becoming cold or indifferent. It means choosing not to absorb everything emotionally.

Practical Steps:

- Ask yourself: "Am I supposed to carry it?"

- Understand emotions without immediately reacting.

- Avoid engaging yourself in every argument or opinion battle.

- Let others have experience to their consequences.

An Invitation

Happiness is not something you earn. You don't have to chase it. You don't have to wait for it.

Peace grows the moment you choose to build it within yourself. So, are you ready to choose peace? This is where chasing chaos ends—and creating happiness begins. Chaos makes us exhausted because it reflects what is not happening by our control.

Instead, shift the focus to:

- Your reactions

- Your habits

- Your boundaries

- Your attitude

- Your beliefs

Daily question:

> "What is the one thing that can be done today to
> support my peace?"

Turning Inward

We often believe that our joy is a reaction to the world around us. But this approach causes us to live life with a fragile footing because the world is unpredictable. If your happiness depends on praise, wealth, or specific outcomes, you are being held hostage by fortune. When we shift the focus inward, we stop asking the world to **"make"** us happy and instead start having a sense of peace that exists independently of our to-do lists or bank accounts. This doesn't mean we become indifferent to life. Rather, we become emotionally self-reliant. Life cannot be predicted. Inner happiness keeps us grounded during challenges, failures, or uncertainty. When happiness comes from within, setbacks are less hurtful, and recovery is faster.

Joy that arises from the world around us can feel bright and electric, especially in the age of social media.

We scroll for connection, inspiration, or a spark of happiness, and sometimes we find it. But when joy depends on likes, comments, and comparisons, it becomes fragile and fleeting. One post can make us feel on top of the world, and the next can knock us flat, reminding us of what we don't have or who we have yet to become. Hours slip away, the day gets swallowed, and instead of living our own story, we watch everyone else's unfold online. Social media promises joy, but too often it steals it, leaving us empty and wondering where our time and peace went.

But once we realize how easily joy can be stolen, especially by the endless pull of social media, we start to see the truth. The world will endlessly tug at our attention or try to minimize our sense of self-worth, but we have the power to stop chasing validation on screens and start grounding ourselves.

Why These Patterns Reduce Happiness

- Idealism makes others feel inadequate.

- It causes anxiety about what others are doing and what we are missing out on.

- Constant pressure of being relevant increases stress and low mood.

- Social standards and feedback trigger dopamine cycles, tying happiness to engagement.

◆ Sleep disruption and distraction disrupt focus and cause emotional imbalance.

These psychological pathways help to explain why prolonged social engagements often lead to emotional costs, even when users think they are enjoying themselves.

The path to true happiness begins with embracing who you are—the unfiltered version of you that exists outside of the scroll. When we return to ourselves, the joy stops being something we find online and becomes something we carry within us. People who work on inner happiness tend to worry less about results that they cannot control. This reduces chronic stress, improves mental health, and supports a much calmer nervous system.

> *"For I have learned to be content whatever the circumstances . . .*
> *I have learned the secret of being content."*
>
> Philippians 4:11–12 (NIV)

Happiness rooted in God is not shaken by external circumstances. In place of relying on others for validation and contentment, try praying. Inner happiness acts like emotional armor. You can face criticism, loss, or failure without losing your sense of worth or hope. This resilience is key to long-term success.

While a sunny day is pleasant, true contentment comes from building a shelter within ourselves that can withstand any storm. Persistent exhaustion from over-functioning, carrying responsibility for others, and trying to be everything to everybody can lead to burnout from self-neglect. When you are internally satisfied, you make decisions based on clarity and your values rather than fear, insecurity, or desperation. This leads to healthier relationships and life paths.

Self-healing serves as medicine, helping people feel seen, heard, and loved. Prioritize rest and self-care to restore your ability to be present and maintain your health. Inner happiness increases focus, motivation, and creativity. People who feel emotionally content work better, solve problems more effectively, and experience less burnout.

Other people can't fill your internal hole, and it's unfair to expect this. When you are internally happy, you don't depend on others to "complete" you. This reduces conflict, jealousy, and emotional dependence, allowing relationships to grow on respect and understanding.

Allow space for God and stop getting in the way of His deliverance. Go rest, go eat, go breathe. We are tired because we try to do what only God can do. Stop merely surviving. A Pew Research Center analysis across 26 countries found that people who identify as spiritual report higher levels of life satisfaction, gratitude, and emotional stability than their non-spiritual counterparts.

Take care of yourself: **Place boundaries, release over-responsibility, schedule rest**, and **nourish yourself** through food.

True happiness begins with the realization that our thoughts create our reality. Happiness is found in:

♦ **Self-Acceptance:** Embracing who you are today rather than who you think you should be.

♦ **Mindfulness:** Learning to exist in the present moment rather than ruminate on the past or fear the future.

♦ **Gratitude:** Shifting the lens from what is **"missing"** to what we have.

By focusing on self-acceptance, mindfulness, and gratitude, we begin to produce our own **"fuel."** This focus transforms happiness from a fleeting emotion triggered by luck into a practiced skill.

Ultimately, believing that happiness begins within is an act of self-empowerment. It means that even in difficult times, you retain the ability to choose your response. You can't always control what happens to you, but you can control the story you build around it. When you stop looking "out there" for a spark and start tending to the fire "in here," you find a steady source of warmth that no circumstance can truly extinguish.

The idea that happiness is an inside job takes on an even deeper meaning when we view it through the lens of faith. In this light, "inside" doesn't just refer to our psychology, but to the dwelling place of the Spirit. We often exhaust ourselves chasing societal milestones, hoping they will fill the quiet aches in our hearts. Yet, from a faith-based perspective, these external things are just shadows. Real, unshakable joy isn't something we stumble upon in the world; it is a gift already planted within us, waiting to be nurtured through our relationship with God.

We often mistake **"happiness"—our current feelings**—for joy, which is anchored to God's promises. When we believe that fulfillment is an "inside job," we acknowledge that while the world is chaotic and shifting, God's word is constant. If our peace is built on the foundation of God's love, it cannot be shaken by a bad week, a lost job, or a difficult relationship. We stop using our bank accounts or our followers as barometers of our worth and start looking to our identity as a child of God. This shift moves us from being victims to stewards of our souls.

If joy begins within, then our spiritual beliefs are the tools we use to maintain that thinking. Cultivating this "inside job" involves:

- **Surrender:** Letting go of the need to control outcomes and trusting in God's plan.

- **Prayer:** Silencing the noise of the world to hear the small voice that reminds us we are enough.

- **Purpose:** Recognizing that our joy is magnified when we use our gifts to help others, reflecting light outward.

By focusing on the heart—**the place where God meets us**—we find that we no longer need to "get" anything from the world to feel whole. We are already living from a place of abundance.

A faith-based joy serves as an anchor. The Bible speaks of a **"peace that passes all understanding,"** which is the definition of an inside job. It is a peace that doesn't make sense to the outside observer because it persists even in the valley. When we realize that God is within us, we stop begging for validation from the world. We realize that the fire we've been looking for wasn't something we had to light ourselves; it was a flame placed in our hearts by God, meant to burn even when the wind is blowing around us.

Chapter 2:

Choosing Joy on Purpose

J oy is not a coincidence—it is a choice. Not a passive hope or a lucky break, but a daily decision to participate in your own happiness. Most people treat joy like a surprise visitor. It shows up when life is smooth and disappears when it's messy. But joy isn't something you find. Joy is something you practice.

The Myth of "Someday"

We often imagine that someday we'll have more peace, life will feel easier, or more enjoyable. But someday never arrives on its own. There will always be stress, responsibility, imperfection, disappointment, and seasons of overwhelm.

Joy cannot wait until life behaves. Joy must be chosen right where you are.

Joy in the Small Decisions

Joy grows in micro-moments, such as:

- Pausing before reacting
- Smiling at something simple
- Letting yourself laugh
- Enjoying your coffee without rushing
- Taking a breath instead of spiraling
- Choosing curiosity over criticism
- Learning to walk away

Joy is ordinary, not extraordinary—and that is what makes it accessible every day.

Positive psychology research led by Dr. Barbara Fredrickson demonstrates that tiny positive emotions such as gratitude, amusement, love, and curiosity enhance our thinking and construct psychological resilience over time. This is known as the "Broaden-and-Build Theory." Even brief moments of positive emotion strengthen coping ability and long-term well-being.

Daily Practice:

Each night, write down three small things that went well and what made them happen. This practice increases happiness and reduces depressive symptoms when done consistently for 2 weeks.

Set the Tone on Purpose

Many people begin the day already defeated: checking messages, scrolling social media, absorbing stress, and rushing into something.

But imagine setting your morning with intention. This could look like:

♦ A breath before your feet hit the floor

♦ A whispered prayer

♦ A thought like, "Today, I choose peace."

♦ A note of gratitude

One of the most effective ways to intentionally set this tone is through positive self-talk. The words you say to yourself at the beginning of the morning become the emotional shadow for your day. Your self-talk directly influences your emotions, stress levels, confidence, and even behaviors. According to cognitive behavioral theory, feelings drive our thoughts, and behavior drives our feelings. When your inner voice is negative, rushed, or submissive, your body releases tension and stress hormones. When your inner voice is gentle, encouraging, and hopeful, your nervous system responds with effective regulation and resilience. Neuroscience also suggests that repetitive positive thoughts can, through neuroplasticity, eventually reconnect neural pathways, strengthening patterns of optimism and emotional balance. In simple words: the way you speak to yourself becomes the way your brain learns to respond to life.

Impact of Positive Self-Talk:

- You become less anxious and have reduced stress as the threat response in the brain gets calmer.

- Your self-confidence and resilience are built while coping with challenges.

- Your focus and productivity are enhanced.

- Your emotional regulation becomes better.

- You become confident through healthier decision-making

Practical Ways to Build Positive Self-Talk:

- Catch the Critic by noticing the negative automatic thoughts, such as "It can't be done by me" or "I'm not enough." Awareness is the first step.

- Reframe these negative thoughts gently with realistic, empowering ones.

  Instead of: **"I am emotionally dependent."** try: **"I can handle whatever comes step by step."**

- Create a morning anchor phase and repeat it daily.

  - **"I am stable and calm."**

  - **"Today, I choose myself."**

  - **"I trust the process of healing."**

- Speak to Yourself as You Would to Someone You Love:

If you wouldn't say it to a friend, don't say it to yourself.

Over time, positive self-talk is not about ignoring difficulties; it is about cultivating a supportive inner companion rather than a harsh inner critic. When you set the tone internally by breath, prayer, gratitude, and empowering inner words, you are not just starting your day. You are shaping your identity, one thought at a time.

Joy can exist with Pain

Choosing joy doesn't mean ignoring hardship. Real joy says, **"This situation is hard, and I can still experience goodness inside it."**

Joy doesn't ask life to be perfect. It asks you to be present. Joy in difficult times doesn't expect you to laugh every day. It means you do not let the darkness define your identity.

You can pause and still carry hope.

You can strive and still be grateful.

You can be in a thunderstorm and still believe in sunrise.

Reflection Questions

- ◆ What brought me even a minute of comfort today?

- ◆ What strength has this difficult time revealed in me?

- ◆ If this season had a lesson, what might it be?

- How would the strongest version of me walk through this?

Stop Outsourcing Happiness

When joy depends on someone else's approval or behavior, a perfect day, or everything going right, you give away your power. But when you choose joy, when you recognize that it is an inside job, you bring your power back home. You reclaim your power.

You may be outsourcing happiness if your emotional stability is dependent on things outside your control.

Here are clear signs to look for

- Other people's behaviors decide your mood.

- You constantly live in "I'll Be Happy When…"

- Your achievements don't make you happy once you get them.

- You search for a distraction most of the time.

- You doubt your self-worth by your performances.

- You blame external elements for your emotional state.

- You are not ready to take on any emotional stability.

How to stop outsourcing happiness and start generating it from within:

1. Recognize the "When–Then" Trap

Pay attention to thoughts like:

- "I'll be happy when I get engaged."
- "I'll feel peaceful when things settle down."
- "I'll feel worthy when people praise me."
- What "when–then" story am I currently telling myself?

2. Shift from Outcome Goals to Identity Values.

Instead of:

- "I want to be beautiful so I can feel confident."

Try:

- "I choose to be confident being myself."

This moves happiness from destination to identity.

3. Reclaim Emotional Responsibility

When we say:

- "They made me exhausted."
- "This situation ruined my excitement."

We unknowingly give others control.

Between action and reaction, there is a space. That space is your freedom.

Practice saying:

"I feel exhausted, and I choose how to respond."

Permission to Feel Good

Many people feel guilty enjoying life when everything isn't solved yet. But joy doesn't mean that you don't care, that you're not working hard, or that you're ignoring problems.

Joy is fuel, not avoidance. It gives you the strength to face life's challenges.

Feeling good in all the given circumstances doesn't mean being happy all the time. It means developing emotional steadiness; the ability to access peace, meaning, or strength even in difficulty.

Here's how:

1. Separate Pain from Suffering

Pain is natural.

Suffering is often the story we add.

Example:

Fact: **"This proposal failed."**

Story: **"I am a failure."**

2. Shift from Control to Response

You become miserable by trying to control what isn't controllable.

Instead ask:

- What can I control right now?

- What kind of person do I need to be in this moment?

A Powerful Reframe Instead of asking:

- "How do I become happy in any circumstance?"

Try:

- "How do I stay wired with who I want to be, regardless of circumstances?"

That question changes everything.

Joy Takes Courage

It takes courage to:

- Slow down

- Be content

- Enjoy yourself without apology

- Celebrate small wins

- Choose gratitude instead of stress

- Look for light in ordinary days

In a world addicted to chaos, joy is rebellion.

A New Definition

Joy is not a prize at the finish line. Joy is the way you travel. It doesn't come from perfection but from participation.

Choosing joy is choosing life: fully, intentionally, imperfectly, and beautifully. Joy is happiness.

> *"This is the day the Lord has made; we will rejoice and be glad in it."*
>
> Psalm 118:24 (NKJK)

Joy is not accidental; it is a daily spiritual decision. We often wait for joy to show up, thinking it will arrive when the schedule evens out, when the crisis calms, when life finally behaves. But the Bible never tells us to wait for joy; it invites us to choose it. When we choose joy with intention, we step into a truth God has already declared over us, and that is:

> *"The joy of the Lord is our strength."*
>
> Nehemiah 8:10

Joy becomes less about how well things are going around us and more about how grounded we are in Him. When we choose joy, we are declaring our trust in God. It is an act of faith that God's goodness is greater than our mess and that peace is possible right in the middle of it.

Choosing joy on purpose means waking up and aligning yourself with heaven before the world has a chance to pull you off course. It means deciding whose voice gets to lead your day: the ceaseless tugs of anxiety, disappointment, and pressure, or God's whisper of hope, peace, and purpose. Joy doesn't ignore pain, forget your struggle, or deny the truth. Joy exists with hard things because it's rooted in something stronger: the presence of God within you. Joy says if life feels uncertain, God is with me. It is a bold, daily choice to believe God is working in all things, even the ones you don't understand yet. And when you choose joy on purpose, you allow God's strength, His calm, and His goodness to seep into every corner of your day, one decision at a time.

Joy doesn't just appear like the sunrise; it is in the heart of a believer. Scripture never suggests joy is a feeling reserved for the lucky ones. It is rooted in knowing who God is. Really knowing Him by talking to Him and spending time with Him in prayer. When we choose joy on purpose, we open our hands and say, **"I trust you more than this part of this story."** We anchor ourselves to the truth that the joy of the Lord is not just pleasant— it is our strength. This kind of joy doesn't happen with circumstances. It flows from the presence of a God who holds our past, present, and future in His hands.

But choosing joy becomes especially powerful when worry comes knocking. Worry is one of the enemy's favorite tools—it whispers worst-case scenarios, magnifies uncertainty, and convinces us that fear is needed. We find ourselves rehearsing problems, "borrowing trouble" from tomorrow, and replaying conversations that haven't even happened. Anxiety tells us we must hold everything together.

"Cast all your cares on Him, for He cares for you."

Peter 5:7

When we wallow in fear, we exhaust ourselves by trying to solve situations we can't control, or fix people God never asked us to fix. This emotional whirlwind creates chaos, not joy. We overthink issues and make them bigger problems by worrying.

Worry steals today's peace by dragging us into what ifs. It turns our mind into a minefield and our spirit into a storm. We become so busy anticipating what might happen that we miss what God is holding together. Anxious thoughts rarely stay small; they multiply and crowd out the voice of God. Before we realize it, we are living in made-up disasters instead of present blessings. Worry is the habit of rehearsing things that have not happened, spending emotional energy on futures that may never arrive. This robs us of the blessings that actually exist in the present moment where life is still whole and grace is at work.

"Do not worry about tomorrow, for tomorrow will worry about itself."

Matthew 6:34

God already stands in every future moment we fear: equipped, capable, victorious.

Choosing joy on purpose is choosing to step out of that storm and into the hands of God. It means interrupting the spiral, refusing to let fear design our day, and returns our attention to His goodness. Joy acknowledges the hard things, but it refuses to hand them the mic. **Joy says, "I don't know how this will work out, but I know who is working in it."** When we choose joy, we loosen our grip on worry and tighten our grip on God's promises.

This is where peace begins: not in perfect circumstances, but in surrendered hearts. The world teaches us to panic, plan, and control, but God invites us to pray, trust, and rest.

The more we choose joy, the quicker we recognize when we're heading into mental chaos. We begin to feel the difference between a life driven by worry and a life driven by God's presence.

Every single day offers the same crossroads: Fear or faith. Chaos or calm. Borrowed trouble or borrowed grace. Reaction or response. Worry or worship. Habit or holiness.

Joy will never bully its way in, but it will always answer when called on. And when you choose joy, you are choosing not just happiness but the God who already sees victory on the other side of your story.

Chaos rarely barges into our lives fully formed. It sneaks in through patterns, habits, and small choices that seem harmless at first. Most of us don't mean to create chaos; we simply live busy lives. We say yes without thinking, react instead of reflect, rush instead of breathe, solve instead of surrender, and worry instead of trust.

Chaos grows in the spaces where we:

- Overcommit because we fear disappointing someone

- Overthink because we don't feel safe letting go

- Over-function because we doubt God will show up

- Over-give because we feel responsible for everyone

- Over-scroll because quietness feels uncomfortable

- Overreact because of being triggered

- Overanalyze because we're afraid of being wrong

One choice at a time, we create a life that is louder than our soul can handle. Chaos isn't just busyness—it's emotional hustle. It's the constant background hum of:

- "I should be doing more."

- "Everyone depends on me; easier to do it myself."

- "What if everything falls apart if I stop?"

- "What will they think if I say no?"

Chaos is born the moment we believe the weight of the world is ours to carry. But here's the truth: Chaos is something we participate in, which means it is also something we can step out of.

Choosing happiness doesn't mean ignoring reality; it means deciding what reality gets to shape you. Happiness begins with a shift: from reaction to intention, from pressure to purpose, from constant doing to meaningful being, from fixing to trusting, from self-neglect to self-stewardship. Instead of frantically believing that you have to do everything, choosing happiness flames the inner knowing that God already has the outcome handled. Choosing happiness is choosing peace over adrenaline. God never asked us to live frantic or fragmented lives.

Jesus said, "My peace I give you, not as the world gives."

John 14:27

The world gives chaos. Jesus gives calm. Happiness takes shape when you:

- Use no as a complete sentence

- Pause before reacting

- Create margins instead of living at the edge

- Let others feel their own consequences

- Trust God with what you can't control

- Give yourself permission to rest without apology

Happiness is not a reward at the end of a perfect day. It is the gift that comes when your spirit finally gets room to breathe. Happiness is rooted in the truth: **"God is with me." "God cares."**

Chapter 3:

LET GO TO GROW

Growth isn't always about learning more, doing more, or becoming more. Sometimes the most important growth requires releasing what you were never meant to carry. Letting go isn't weakness—it's wisdom. It's recognizing that you can't step fully into your next season while dragging the weight of the last one.

Letting go isn't about releasing something randomly, but it's about getting rid of what is costing you more than it's giving you.

Here's how you can know what you need to let go of:

- Notice what drains your energy.
- Identify fear-based attachments.
- Notice what is stopping you from growing up.
- Look at what triggers your emotions repeatedly.

Letting go doesn't always mean walking away.

It can mean:

♦ Releasing unnecessary expectations.

♦ Releasing control of others to your life.

♦ Releasing resentment.

♦ Releasing the need for constant validation from others.

♦ Releasing the past shadow from your present.

Sometimes we let go internally first, and that changes everything later.

A Simple Self-Reflection Practice

Write this sentence and complete it honestly:

"I know I need to let go of _________________because it makes me feel _______________."

The Weight You Can't See

Imagine running full speed while dragging a heavy load behind you. Even if you're strong, eventually you will collapse—not because you failed, but because you were overloaded. Straining forward while hauling the weight of the past. That's how life works, too.

Letting go of the past is not about losing your memory. It's about ending its control over your present days because the past is one of the biggest delusions where we outsource our emotional state. We don't hold on to events.

We hold on to:

♦ Our interpretation of those events

♦ The idea we construct around those events

♦ The emotions we never regulate

For Example:

"It happened" becomes **"It happened because I never tried enough."** That second part is what needs to be removed.

Practice:

Take one painful memory and write two columns:

Facts (Objective)	Story (Interpretation)
Painful Memory / Incident	What you concluded about yourself because of it.

Most suffering lives in Column 2.

Letting go means rewriting the interpretation, not denying the event.

Reflection question:

"If my friend had made this mistake, would I condemn them forever?"

We carry limiting beliefs, outdated identities, outgrown relationships, and guilt and shame from past mistakes. These invisible weights drain us far more than anything physical ever could. Letting go is not a quick achievement. It's an everyday choice. Somedays you'll feel free. Some days, the memory will resurface. Progress is when the memory becomes information, not the shadows of yourself.

Why Letting Go Feels So Hard

Letting go sounds simple until you face what needs releasing. Hidden inside every burden is something familiar:

- A belief that once protected you

- A relationship that once mattered deeply

- A role you once relied on

- A coping mechanism that helped you survive

- A dream that made sense in the past

- A painful emotion you had buried

Letting go requires allowing yourself to evolve, and this always feels a little like loss. Fears arise even when you're releasing something painful, but holding onto what hurts guarantees stagnation. Letting go opens space for new life.

Reflection question:

Instead of asking:

♦ "Why is this still hurting?"

Ask:

♦ "What did this loss teach me about what I value?"

That question begins the shift from suffering to learning.

What Letting Go Actually Means

Letting go is not forgetting, denying, pretending, or invalidating what once mattered. Letting go means to:

♦ Remove its power over your present.

♦ Release attachment, not the lesson.

♦ Accept that some chapters must close.

♦ Allow room for something new to grow.

♦ Sit with emotions to feel them.

You don't erase your story—you heal it. You keep the wisdom, not the wound.

When the Past Follows You

Sometimes you let go mentally but still carry it emotionally. You may leave the relationship but keep the guilt, quit the job but bring the stress home, move forward but replay the memories, or outgrow the role but cling to the identity of the hurt or betrayal.

Release is often a process, not a switch. Some things fall away quickly, while others loosen slowly like tangled threads. Be gentle with yourself. Growth rarely moves in a straight line. Take your wins, no matter how small.

Daily practice:

Take 3 deep breaths and name any 3 things you're grateful for. Take one small action aligned with your future self.

Grief as a Sign of Growth

Letting go brings grief—not just for who or what you're leaving, but for who you were. You may grieve:

- Time spent trying to make trust work

- An expectation that didn't unfold

- A version of yourself who tried her best

- A dream you're no longer called to pursue

- A friendship you outgrew and had to leave

Grief doesn't mean you failed. It means you're changing.

Practical exercise:

Set a timer for 15 minutes. Write about your emotional experiences without stopping or editing. Don't try to sound wise. Just empty it. Then close the notebook. You are processing your emotions, not living there permanently.

Making Room for What's Meant for You

Empty spaces never stay empty for long. When you let go of something, space opens, and God has a beautiful way of filling empty spaces with better things.

But nothing new can enter a life that is already stuffed full. This means that to receive peace, you must release chaos. To receive love, you must release fear. To receive confidence, you must release self-doubt. To receive alignment, you must release forcing. And to receive joy, you must release resentment. To feel safe, you must release control to God.

Clearing space is an act of bravery. Imagine your hands are full of pebbles. Even if someone offers you flowers, you can't receive them. Letting go is not about dropping something worthy. It's about freeing your hands.

When you let go:

- Your thinking becomes more sensible.

- Your creativity booms.

- ◆ It improves your decision-making process.

- ◆ Letting go rephrases self-perception:

  - ◊ "I'm resilient."

  - ◊ "I'm improving."

  - ◊ "I'm enough."

Trusting the Subtraction

We live in a world obsessed with more: more money, more followers, more of everything. But sometimes, more is the problem.

Letting go is courageous because it asks you to trust that you are enough without adding anything else. Your life can expand by having less, not more. When you clear the clutter, you actually have more access. Clearing clutter makes clarity.

The problem isn't having the excess. The problem is believing: **"More will finally make me feel valuable."** That belief is draining.

A Rebalancing Question

Instead of asking:

- ◆ "How can I get more?"

Ask:

- ◆ "What actually adds value to my life?"

- ◆ "What gives me energy instead of draining it?"

A New Identity Emerges

When you loosen your grip on what weighs you down, something extraordinary happens:

◆ Your voice grows clearer

◆ Your spirit becomes lighter

◆ Your decisions become wiser

◆ Your joy becomes truer

◆ Your confidence rises

◆ Your future expands

You begin to meet the version of yourself who's been waiting beneath the heaviness. Letting go isn't an ending. Letting go is a doorway.

Try:

◆ Write what you're letting go of and burn the paper.

◆ Pray and consciously believe in it.

◆ Donate something that relates to the old chapter.

◆ Change your environment (hair, room, routine, etc.)

The brain reacts strongly to routine. It signals transition.

A Gentle Invitation

Take inventory of what you're carrying—physically, emotionally, spiritually. Ask yourself, "Does this support who I'm becoming, or does it hold me back?" Your answer may feel surprising or obvious.

Letting go requires trust. Trust in God. Trust in your growth. Trust that more life, more freedom, and more peace are ahead of you. Choose release, not because it's easy, but because you deserve the space that opens when you do. This is a difficult task. My recent tangle with skin cancer on my nose was humbling. The surgeon explained that it went deep, about an inch long, and the stitches traveled from my eye to the bottom of my nose. I had to trust his work because not removing the cancer was not an option. I had to trust God and wait for my black eyes and suture lines to heal. Once again, I was set apart to write, pray, plan, and rest. We don't always understand the path God is taking us on, but sometimes it is exactly what we need to give us everything we always wanted. I kept praying, "God, I want to know you." And now I'm homebound until this swelling in my nose goes down and I'm forced to rest.

I'm delaying recording my next series of podcasts because of this speed bump. We live in a world that doesn't want to see a nose full of stitches, swelling, and bruises.

Life always has speed bumps and interruptions we don't expect. It's not about avoiding the bumps; it's about how we get back up and navigate through them.

Let's go to grow. Your next season is waiting.

*"Forget the former things; do not dwell on the past.
See, I am doing a new thing!"*

Isaiah 43:18–19 (NIV)

Growth requires letting go of what keeps you rooted in yesterday. Some of the most important growth we ever experience is not from what we gain, but from what we release. Letting go is rarely easy. In fact, it's often painful and almost always misunderstood from the outside. Yet, it is one of the most spiritually courageous things a person can do.

We are taught to hold on, to fight harder, to give more, to stay longer. We take pride in loyalty, endurance, and sacrifice. But not everything we cling to was meant to survive every season of our lives.

Sometimes the very thing we're gripping tight—the relationship, the role, the belief, the pain—is the very thing choking out our ability to grow. Loosening your grip is the first step in moving forward.

Letting go becomes an act of survival. An act of clarity. An act of trust. An act of obedience to God.

Reflection for You

Ask yourself quietly:

◆ What am I holding more firmly than my trust in God?

◆ If I truly believed God is holding onto me, what would I release today?

♦ What if letting go is not weakness but its own kind of worship?

Releasing Old Relationships

One of the hardest things to release is our relationships that once felt like home, especially emotionally damaging ones. Take a narcissistic relationship, for example. At first, it may feel magnetic, comforting, or necessary. But your beliefs around the relationship may be limiting. You may believe they really love and need you, or that you can help them change. You may take responsibility for their unhappiness.

Narcissistic relationships are built on confusion and chaos, where love is mixed with manipulation, affection is paired with criticism, and closeness is shadowed by control.

You begin to shrink to stay small enough not to upset them. You make yourself quieter, more accommodating. You swallow your needs out of fear of triggering their moods. You apologize for hurting their feelings, even when you're bleeding emotionally.

Little by little, you become lost in your own life. And it feels impossible to walk away. You hide this from others because of shame.

Letting go of a toxic relationship may feel like ripping out a piece of your own heart. Not because the relationship was good and nourishing, but because it dug roots so deep into you that you hardly know who you are without it.

So while releasing the narcissistic relationship means letting go to reclaim your power, you also grieve:

♦ The version of them they sold you

♦ The promises they made

♦ The life you believed in

♦ The time you invested

♦ The hope that you could change them

♦ The identity you formed around being needed and chosen

Even abuse can feel familiar when it's been normalized long enough. And the familiar can look like safety even when it's destroying you. It's confusing.

Letting go isn't just the end of a relationship; it is the death of an old version of you. Growth begins the moment you whisper to yourself: **"This is not love"** or **"I can't survive here anymore."** It doesn't matter if it is a friend, a boss, or an Aunt... if the person leaves you drained and feeling bad, why endure this relationship?

Often, there isn't an obvious moment but instead a series of small awakenings: the apology that doesn't come, the betrayal cloaked in excuses, the constant devaluation of your feelings, and the stark realization that you've abandoned yourself in the process— the slow build-up of contempt.

Then one morning, you wake up feeling more exhausted to stay than afraid to leave. This is the turning point. Know God is standing with you.

Leaving a narcissistic relationship isn't a weakness. It is a strength clothed in shaking hands. It requires:

♦ Choosing truth over illusion

♦ Stepping away from control and manipulation

♦ Standing up for yourself

♦ Angering someone who expects you to stay silent

♦ Walking into uncertainty with nothing but faith

And when you leave, they often try to lure you back through **guilt**, **nostalgia**, or fear. **Financial abuse** and **emotional abuse continue**. But healing lives on the other side of the door you finally had the strength and courage to close. I know: It happened to me.

Before You Leave: Strengthen Yourself Quietly

Do this first:

♦ Get the needed emotional support (trusted friend, family, and therapist).

♦ Take the sharing to minimal levels.

♦ Start mental detachment before physically leaving.

PART II: CALMING THE NOISE

Chapter 4:

The Calm You Create

Most people believe calm is something that just happens. They imagine peace as a place they'll arrive at when life finally cooperates: when the schedule lightens, when people get easier, when circumstances are less demanding.

But calm is rarely something you find. Calm is something you build, deliberately, thoughtfully, and one choice at a time. Calm is a practiced state of mind.

The Myth of a Calm Life

Many of us wait for calmness, like it's coming right around the corner. We expect life to settle down eventually. But it doesn't. Life hurries on. Pushes past us.

So if calm is going to exist in your world, it will be because you created it, not because life delivered it. Calm is practiced, not found.

How Calm Feels in Daily Life

♦ You don't make decisions out of fear.

♦ You don't need a constant validation.

♦ You don't over-explain yourself to others.

♦ You live with fewer mental battles.

♦ You trust that what's meant for you will eventually find you.

Chaos as the Default

Chaos is easy. Without intention, we:

♦ Say yes when we mean no.

♦ Lose control of our schedules.

♦ Find ourselves in unwanted drama.

♦ Take on other people's responsibilities.

Chaos becomes the default mode. Calm, however, requires conscious interruption.

Calm Is Not Laziness

Somewhere along the way, slowing down began to feel like slacking off. We were taught that being busy meant we were important, productive, and valuable. We were taught to base our value on our accomplishments. We put ourselves last and never recharged our own batteries.

So when we rest, we feel guilty. When we pause, we feel behind. When we breathe, we feel irresponsible. But calm isn't laziness. Calm is stewardship. It is about managing your body, mind, heart, and energy, and paying attention to your relationships and spirit.

A calm life is not an empty one. A calm life is an intentional one.

What Calm Is NOT

- Not being emotionless

- Not suppressing feelings

- Not avoiding responsibility

- Not pretending everything is fine

Calm is strength, not numbness.

The Power of the Pause

Every calm life begins with a pause. A pause before you react. A pause before you agree. A pause before you rush in to fix. A pause before you say yes when you mean no.

That tiny space between what you want and what you do is where your power lives.

And sometimes you forget what you want because you stopped asking yourself, so you really don't know what you actually want.

Ask yourself, **"Will this cost me more peace than it's worth?"** Often, the answer is yes.

A Gentle Reframe

Instead of:

♦ "I'm wasting my time doing nothing."

Try:

♦ "I am regulating my nervous system."
♦ "I am building emotional stability."
♦ "I am protecting my inner peace."

That is strength, not laziness.

A Question for You

When you slow down, whose voice calls you lazy? Is it truly yours… or someone you learned it from?

That awareness alone brings freedom.

Calm in Your Environment

Your environment can support your nervous system, or stress it out. Calm grows in spaces that breathe. Calm spaces include a clear countertop, a made bed, and a streamlined closet.

You don't need a magazine-perfect house. Just a space that tells your body, "You're safe here." External calm nourishes internal calm. You don't owe anyone unlimited access.

Not everyone or everything is good for you. You can still love people and not lose yourself along the way.

Practice:

In any environment:

♦ Breathe in slowly through the nose. (4 seconds)

♦ Hold. (2–3 seconds)

♦ Breathe out slowly through the mouth. (6 seconds)

Longer exhale activates your nervous system.

Calm in Relationships

Calm isn't only personal. It's also relational. Create calm by stepping away from gossip, leaving the room before your boundaries break, and refusing to participate in chaos.

People can't just come into your life for no reason. The lessons you learn and the growth that you experience are never spontaneous. It's always meant to be because there is a higher purpose.

You don't have to attend every argument you're invited to. Some battles end best when you bow out gracefully. Save your energy for what really matters. Find relationships that mirror your calm and attract peace.

Family is everything, but the requirement isn't blood; it's love, respect, and safety. Family is whoever feels like home to you.

A Powerful Shift

Instead of asking:

♦ "How do I make them change?"

Ask:

♦ "How do I remain calm, not depending on them?"

That's emotional power.

Calm in Your Thoughts

Even with a quiet home and peaceful routines, chaos can live loudly in your mind. Your mind is not a storage unit for other people's chaos. Calm thinking is not the absence of stress. It's the ability to steer your thoughts gently.

Try:

♦ Naming what you can control.

♦ Releasing what you can't into God's hands.

♦ Questioning stories your mind creates.

♦ Offering yourself compassion instead of criticism.

Calm begins where judgment ends.

Boundaries: Calm's Best Friend

Without boundaries, calm is impossible. Boundaries say:

- This is how I protect myself.

- This is what I give access to in my life.

- This is where I stop, this is my hard pass.

Boundaries preserve your energy, clarity, safety, and joy. They create the quiet needed for peace to grow.

Calm in Stormy Seasons

Calm doesn't promise ease. It promises steadiness. Hard seasons still come. Storms still break over your life. But calm reminds you that you don't have to be swept away.

Calm looks like:

- Breathing deeply instead of spiraling.

- Taking things one moment at a time.

- Letting go of what today can't hold.

- Whispering, **"God cares."**

Calm is your anchor, not your escape.

Calm Becomes Who You Are

The more you practice calm, the softer your relationships become and the more your nervous system relaxes. Your priorities sharpen, and decisions become clearer. Overall, joy is easier to access.

Calm stops being something you chase and becomes something you embrace. Chaos may still knock, but you no longer rush to greet it like an old friend.

A New Way Forward

You don't stumble into peace. You choose it. Over and over. Sometimes quietly. Sometimes fiercely. And as you repeatedly choose calm, your life makes more sense. Your body feels safer. Your days feel lighter. Your relationships feel secure. Your happiness becomes sustainable.

You become the leader of your environment, not a victim of it.

Calm is not an accident. Calm is a creation. And you—far more than anyone else—are the artist of your life.

> *"Peace I leave with you; my peace I give you . . .*
> *Do not let your hearts be troubled and do not be*
> *afraid."*
>
> John 14:27 (NIV)

Jesus offers peace that the world cannot give. Feeling calm begins with Him.

A Woman's Peace

Our society scrutinizes women from the moment we take our first breath. Barely healed from childbirth, new mothers are bombarded with messages about **"getting their body back"**—as if motherhood erased something instead of adding something breathtakingly divine.

Before the baby has even taken their first steps, the mother is already expected to shrink, tone, tighten, smooth, and return to an image of a woman she no longer is, nor is meant to be. "Mommy makeovers," which are surgeries to restore looks, flatten stomachs, and erase stretch marks, have become normalized. Instead of honoring the miracle her body performed—growing and sustaining life—society convinces a woman that she must correct, fix, or hide every mark that proves she was transformed by love.

Middle-aged women are given a different script, but the message is just as damaging:

◆ Aging is a problem to solve.

◆ Wrinkles are flaws to erase.

◆ Gray hair is a failure.

◆ Sagging skin is a shame.

◆ A face that shows experience must be "refreshed."

◆ And menopause is framed as the end of beauty—instead of a powerful beginning.

Facelifts, injections, and **fillers** are marketed not as choices but as shared responsibility: "Everybody does it," "Stay viable," "Stay desirable," "Stay visible."

Every time a woman tries to chase a younger version of herself, she confirms the lie society sells: Who you are right now is not enough. And this reinforces a negative feedback loop: compare, criticize, correct.

But the problem isn't the surgery itself. The problem is the insecurity that drives the decision. When beauty becomes a checklist instead of a celebration, women tend to:

♦ Grow anxious about being seen as they are.

♦ Fear aging like it's a disease.

♦ Feel the need to keep up to stay employable

♦ Go into a spiral to maintain a false ideal.

♦ Emotionally exhaust themselves by trying to keep up.

♦ Lose their identity beneath the "improvements."

Instead of chasing joy, peace, and purpose, we chase youth, approval, and a body that refuses to freeze in time. Chaos replaces contentment. Pressure replaces presence. We watch our lives like critics instead of participants.

And the cruel irony? No matter how much we do, it will never be enough for a culture built on dissatisfaction. A culture that screams more.

God did not design women to live terrified of time. Our bodies were meant to evolve with us—to tell our story, not erase it. Every wrinkle is a laugh we lived. Every stretch mark is love written into skin. Every gray hair is wisdom earned the hard way. Every soft place is a sign we have fed, carried, comforted, nurtured, survived, grown, and endured.

Trying to stop aging is like trying to stop being alive. When we chase youth instead of purpose, we slowly lose:

♦ Gratitude for what our bodies can do.

♦ Spiritual focus on who we are becoming.

♦ Emotional energy reserved for meaning.

♦ Confidence in the natural beauty of authenticity.

♦ The peace that comes with acceptance.

♦ The joy that flows from identity in God, not culture.

Our worth was never meant to be measured in the mirror. A woman who embraces her changing body becomes a rebel in the most powerful way. She chooses:

♦ Presence over perfection.

♦ Gratitude over comparison.

♦ Peace over pressure.

♦ Growth over insecurity.

♦ Identity in God over validation from strangers.

♦ Joy in the life she lives instead of the body she maintains.

She refuses to apologize for being real, human, and beautifully alive.

That doesn't mean surgery is wrong. It means motive matters. If a woman chooses something from confidence, joy, and empowerment—that is freedom. But when the choice stems from shame, fear, insecurity, or cultural pressure, it becomes another form of bondage.

You don't have to look younger, be thinner, hide your age, erase your history, or compete with women who have been filtered and edited into fantasy. You were created for joy, purpose, depth, faith, and connection—not performance, perfection, or perpetual youth.

The world will always try to convince you to chase something else: a smoother face, a tighter body, a longer list of procedures. But peace comes when you stop chasing the mirror and start chasing what actually lasts: love, laughter, faith, purpose, experience, wisdom, relationships, God's calling, and the beauty that radiates from a soul at rest.

A face will change. A body will age. But a woman rooted in unconditional worth will bloom in every season and create a life far more beautiful than anything the world could ever sculpt.

The world defines beauty by what can be seen. God defines beauty by what cannot be shaken.

A Powerful Self-Check

When you feel uneasy around others, ask:

- ◆ Am I trying to impress?

- ◆ Am I trying to avoid judgment?

- ◆ Am I abandoning myself to fit in?

- ◆ Calm returns when you stop abandoning yourself.

Culture has narrowed beauty into a checklist: flawless skin, youthful appearance, a toned body. The list goes on and on. Culture says beauty is visible, external, and temporary. It's something you earn, maintain, improve, and preserve. And when you can't keep up, culture is ready to replace you.

Biblical beauty is the opposite. God says beauty is internal, eternal, and freely given.

> *"People judge by outward appearance, but the Lord looks at the heart."*

> 1 Samuel 16:7

Cultural beauty is transactional. It praises you when you conform, pressures you when you age, silences you when you gain weight, and shames you for imperfections. It demands endless maintenance and keeps us in a constant state of comparison, where the goalposts are always moving.

Cultural beauty says, "You will be loved when ..."—when you lose weight, when you fix that wrinkle, when you buy that cream, when you look more like her. It is beauty based on earning. And earned beauty must be earned each day anew.

I was raised by a Somatic narcissist who believed a person's worth was rooted in the shape of their body, an attractive face, and overall physical appearance. Being raised by a father with these traits was deeply damaging because his love and approval were conditional based on my weight, hair, or clothes. I was raised in a world where beauty was treated as perfection and perfection was treated as worth. Perfection is unattainable and leaves you wanting. Appearance was not just noticed—it was measured, admired, and quietly ranked. The unspoken message was clear: being thin meant being valuable, and being valuable meant being loved.

Cultural beauty demands constant proof. It praises what is seen, rewards what photographs well, and withholds approval when age, weight gain, or imperfection appear. It teaches us to monitor ourselves instead of know ourselves, to perform instead of rest, to chase admiration instead of connection. Under this standard, beauty becomes fragile— always at risk of being lost.

Biblical beauty tells a very different story.

Scripture never defines beauty by symmetry, youth, or physical flawlessness. It defines beauty by who a person is becoming, not how they appear. It honors gentleness, faithfulness, humility, strength of character, and a quiet confidence rooted in truth.

Biblical beauty does not expire with time; it deepens.

When beauty is defined culturally, love becomes conditional. When beauty is defined biblically, worth is settled. One asks, Am I still enough if I change? The other answers, you were enough before you were ever seen.

Healing began when I stopped asking the mirror for permission and started asking God who I already was. Cultural beauty made me feel admired but anxious. Biblical beauty made me feel known and at peace. One demanded perfection. The other offered freedom.

Biblical beauty says, **"You are loved now."** Not later. Not when you fix yourself. Not when you match a standard. Now, as the beloved daughter of God.

Biblical beauty is rooted in:

♦ Character and integrity

♦ Kindness and gentleness

♦ Inner strength and God-confidence

♦ Faithfulness, wisdom, and peace

God doesn't admire the face we paint. He delights in the heart He shaped. Biblical beauty isn't something we fight for. It's something we grow into as God transforms us from the inside.

While cultural beauty is fleeting, biblical beauty deepens with time. A woman walking with God becomes:

- Softer in spirit

- Stronger in faith

- Wiser in decisions

- Deeper in compassion

- Calmer in storms

- More radiant with grace

A wrinkle can't erase that. Stretch marks can't dull that. Gray hair can't touch that. Biblical beauty grows brighter the older you become because it is anchored in eternity, not vanity.

Scripture doesn't shame the physical body; God created it with intention. You can:

- Care for your health

- Appreciate your appearance

- Enjoy fashion, makeup, and creativity

- Age gracefully

- And even choose cosmetic enhancements

But the sacred line is this: Your identity must not depend on what the mirror shows. Culture builds insecurity. God builds identity. God invites us into the kind of beauty that doesn't fade or need defending. The kind of beauty that isn't threatened by age or undone by comparison. Beauty that isn't manufactured or for sale.

It's a beauty the world cannot give, and therefore, cannot take away. A woman rooted in God's definition of beauty no longer begs for approval from a world that profits from her insecurity.

She knows that her body is a temple, not a billboard. Her face is a canvas of stories, not a map of flaws. Her worth was decided by the cross, not culture. This is where happiness grows: not in chasing perfection, but in resting securely in who God created her to be.

A Daily Practice

Every night, tell yourself: **"I accept who I was today. I am learning. I am growing. I do not need to be someone else to be worthy."**

Repeat until your body believes it.

Chapter 5:

LESS BUSY, MORE BLISS

In a world that constantly rewards speed, efficiency, and output, it's easy to believe that being busy is the same thing as living a meaningful life. Busy does not equal fulfillment, happiness, or even necessarily productivity.

Busyness can become a hiding place: a distraction, a badge of honor, a shield from uncomfortable feelings, and sometimes, an identity we don't know how to put down.

Studies show:

- Chronic busyness releases more stress.

- Satisfaction levels decline with constant multitasking.

- Overworking is linked with burnout and emotional exhaustion.

The Trap of Busyness

Somewhere along the way, we decided that worthiness is earned through our accomplishments. We applaud overscheduled lives. We admire people who say, **"I'm swamped."** We equate burnout with importance. The busier we are, the more validated we feel.

But there is a cost. Being busy often leaves no room for what truly matters: presence, joy, stillness, play, reflection, connection, and rest.

We can be surrounded by activity and still be emotionally starving. We take on too much and get anxious and overwhelmed. It can feel lonely.

Ask yourself:

- When I'm busy, do I feel involved or drained?
- Am I living, or escaping?
- If everything went quiet for one day, would I feel calm or panic?

When Busy Becomes a Mask

There are many roads that lead to chronic busyness. Some of us stay busy because:

- Stillness feels uncomfortable.
- Silence feels unfamiliar.
- Productivity feels safer than vulnerability.
- We don't want to disappoint anyone.

- We fear stopping long enough to feel.

- We don't like asking for help.

Others stay busy to avoid unwanted emotions, such as loneliness and grief, or to avoid dealing with difficult decisions. Busy becomes a buffer, but buffers eventually suffocate the person they're meant to protect. It's why some people become workaholics, because work is easier than being at home dealing with conflict. Busyness can reduce chaos, but emotional maturity reduces drama.

Instead of quitting busyness, start small:

- 5 minutes without phone.

- Sit with one emotion without fixing it.

- Let someone be upset without solving it.

You are teaching your nervous system:

"Stillness is not dangerous."

The Difference between Full and Overflowing

Your life can be full without being overwhelming. You can have responsibilities and passions without living in a constant state of anxiousness. A full life feels like having purpose, choice, and clear priorities. It is living from a place of alignment and enoughness. But a life that is overflowing feels like chaos and guilt, stress, resentment, and obligation.

A full life nourishes you. An overflowing life drains you and invites in resentment.

Asking the Right Questions

Instead of asking, "How much can I do?" try asking, **"How do I want to feel while doing it?"** Instead of, "What more can I take on?" ask, **"What can I release?"** And instead of assuming every request needs your yes, ask, **"Is this feeding my soul or feeding my stress?"**

It's okay to say no.

The Courage to Slow Down

Slowing down is countercultural. It is a quiet refusal to let urgency control you. Slowing down may be uncomfortable. In slowing down, you may disappoint someone, you may need to say no, and you'll have to confront your real needs.

But slowing down also means that you will hear your inner voice again and discover what matters to you. You'll be better able to enjoy what you already have and to show up more fully in your life by crossing what you really want.

Speed steals life's meaning when it becomes the default. Instead of: "I am worthy because I am busy." Shift toward: **"I am valuable because I exist."** That shift changes everything.

The Art of Saying No

No is one of your greatest tools for a joyful life. No is a boundary, a filter, a protective shield, and a declaration of self-worth.

Every yes lives somewhere: in your calendar, energy, or emotions. When you say yes to everything, you say no to rest, peace, and presence.

No is not selfish. No is sacred. No is permission to have boundaries.

Instead of:

♦ "No means I am difficult."

Shift to:

♦ "No means I am honest."

Every time you say yes when you mean no, you create:

♦ Internal resentment

♦ Emotional exhaustion

♦ Quiet anger

♦ Self-betrayal

Over time, that creates the very **"drama"** you're trying to avoid.

Intention over Activity

A slow life isn't a small life. A calm life isn't an unproductive one. Intention transforms ordinary moments into meaningful ones:

- Cooking becomes nourishment

- Walking becomes meditation

- Play becomes bonding

- Stillness becomes prayer

- Laughter becomes necessary

Busyness scatters your attention. Intention gathers it.

Without intention:

- Busyness becomes escape.

- Productivity becomes an addiction.

- Achievement feels empty.

With intention:

- Even small acts feel powerful.

- Slowing down feels purposeful, not lazy.

- You choose, instead of react.

Relearning Presence

Presence is the antidote to busyness. Presence looks like:

♦ Hearing the sound of your own laughter

♦ Feeling your breath deepen

♦ Noticing the beauty hidden in ordinary moments

♦ Listening fully to someone you love

♦ Choosing to be where your feet are

♦ Focusing attention on what you want

♦ Putting your phone down to experience the present

Happiness is rarely found in the future you're sprinting toward. Instead, it lives in the moment you are currently overlooking.

Making Room for Bliss

Be intentional about removing things from your life that do not serve you, such as obligations that drain you, tasks done out of guilt, people who demand more than they give, and noise that consumes your attention. The healthier you get, the easier chaos is to spot, and once you see it, you can't unsee it. Awareness lets you notice things you couldn't before. Then you're able to observe instead of absorb.

When you remove those drainers, you make space for joy, creativity, curiosity, wonder, and play. You learn to prioritize healing, connection, and rest.

Busy numbs. Bliss awakens.

Intention changes the quality of the same act.

For Example:

♦ Cleaning with stress → draining.

♦ Cleaning with love → nourishing.

♦ Progress for validation → exhausting.

♦ Progress with purpose → energizing.

Same Activity:

♦ Different inner state.

♦ Different emotional outcome.

Intention is invisible — but it transforms everything.

A New Standard

Your life is not meant to be endured. It is meant to be lived. Because Jesus knew what no therapist, no influencer, no self-help book ever says:

Healing doesn't come from feeling better; it comes from following Him.

Not chasing revenge, not replacing the person, not numbing the pain, but surrendering it. Dying to what was and letting go of what broke you so God can give you something unbreakable. Sometimes, the most healing thing He will do is not take away the wound. But walk with you through it while you lean on Him instead of taking advice from the world.

A busy life may impress people, but a joyful life inspires them. You do not owe the world your exhaustion.

When God cuts away the bad fruit, do not chase after it. Trust Him. Stop trying to poison yourself. You do not have to prove your worth by your pace. You have nothing left to earn—only peace to receive.

You are allowed to choose less: rush, noise, obligation, and people-pleasing.

More bliss. Less busy. More life. Less hurry. You deserve a life that feels good, not just one that looks productive. The more healed you get, the more you understand that peace is priceless. You start to see signs of change, like you stop approaching every task like it's an emergency, and you can sit in silence without needing distraction.

> *Then Jesus said, "Come to me, all of you who are weary and carry heavy burdens, and I will give you rest . . . and you will find rest for your souls. For my yoke is easy and my burden is light."*

> Matthew 11:28–30 (NLT):

God calls us out of exhaustion and into soul-level rest.

Truly happy people don't wait for perfect circumstances to enjoy their lives. Happy women laugh easily, stay present, and ask for what they want without apology. They laugh, not because their lives are flawless, but because they've learned that joy is worth protecting.

Laughter is medicine. It loosens fear, interrupts stress, and reminds us that life is meant to be experienced, not endured.

But laughing freely requires safety—something many women have never been granted. Women who have spent years walking on eggshells, managing emotional landmines, or carrying others' burdens often forget how to play, relax, or let their shoulders drop. Some forget to exhale. For them, laughter feels risky, unfamiliar, and even indulgent.

Learning to laugh again is a reclamation of joy and a declaration that happiness is allowed here. Happy women are present. They show up in their moments instead of rushing through them. They taste their coffee instead of gulping it and breathe deeply instead of bracing for the next crisis.

But presence goes against everything society conditions women to be, which are multitaskers, problem-solvers, emotional caretakers, and anticipators of everyone else's needs. We are rewarded for doing, not being.

So slowing down to feel, enjoy, and exist can feel uncomfortable, even irresponsible. Presence takes practice. It requires untangling from busyness, silencing outside noise, and believing your worth isn't tied to what you produce.

Happy women ask for what they want: love, help, space, time, support, rest, desire, and opportunity. They don't apologize for having needs or dreams. But asking is where most women freeze. We've been trained to take what we're given without rocking the boat.

We've been conditioned to avoid being "too much," to earn everything we receive.

So instead of asking, we hint, hope, over-give, stay silent, or wait for someone to notice what we need. Silence becomes a habit, and resentment becomes the cost.

Asking for what you want is an act of self-respect. Receiving what you ask for is an act of self-worth. Laughing, being present, and asking boldly are not signs of a carefree life—they are signs of a healed one. Asking boldly and being open to receive requires clarity, confidence, boundaries, inner safety, and emotional maturity. It requires trust in God's provision and an anchored belief that your life matters too.

And that is why happy women feel different when they walk into a room. They shine, not because everything is easy, but because they finally know: "I am worthy of joy, and I will not apologize for living it."

Chapter 6:

From Overthinking to Understanding

Your mind can be your greatest ally—or your loudest critic. Overthinking is one of the most common ways we drain our energy, erode our peace, and talk ourselves out of joy.

Most of us weren't taught how to handle our thoughts. We marinate in anxious thoughts, having been taught only how to react to them.

This chapter invites you to step into a new way of relating to your mind, not by shutting it down, but by listening differently.

The Noise in Your Head

Overthinking can take many forms. It can feel like:

- ◆ Replaying conversations

- ◆ Imagining what might go wrong

- ◆ Trying to predict the future

- ◆ Worrying about what someone thinks

- ◆ Analyzing every detail of a situation

- ◆ Rehearsing conversation over and over

It makes us feel responsible, prepared, or cautious. But in reality, overthinking often creates more problems than it prevents. It is worry disguised as wisdom. And it's a destructive time-waster because most of what we worry about never comes to pass.

Reflection:

When you overthink, is it mostly about:

- ◆ The past?

- ◆ The future?

- ◆ Or what others think of you?

A Brain Wired for Protection

Your brain is not trying to stress you out. It's trying to protect you. Your mind naturally scans for danger and tries to prevent future harm. It pushes away past trauma, seeking certainty and closure.

The brain assumes that if I worry about it enough, I can control the outcome.

But thinking doesn't equal control. Understanding this brings relief: You're not failing; you're wired to survive.

Ask yourself:

Is this something I can act on right now?

- If **yes** → write one small action and do it.
- If **no** → this is a mental rehearsal, not problem-solving.

Worry feels productive. But if there is no action attached, it's just looping.

When Thinking Turns Into Overthinking

Thinking, of course, is a helpful process. It brings clarity and helps you solve a problem or develop a plan. Clear thinking leads to clear action.

Overthinking takes over when you get stuck in loops, unable to make a decision. Overthinking is when you jump to imagining worst-case scenarios, and your anxiety grows. Thoughts can feel like storms you can't escape from, and you may even lose sleep because you can't turn them off. That stays in your nervous system, then turns into burnout, which is disguised as perfectionism. This is from being way too hard on yourself when you're already carrying more than most. You don't have to perform without a safety net.

Thinking produces answers. Overthinking produces anxiety.

Purpose Test

Thinking asks:

- "What's the next step?"

Overthinking asks:

- "What if something goes wrong?"

Thinking solves. Overthinking seeks certainty.

A Simple Rule

If it leads to:

- **Clarity** → it's thinking.
- **Confusion** → it's overthinking.

The Stories We Believe

Your brain tells stories, often without your permission. Thoughts like:

- "I feel embarrassed because I said that."

- "I really messed that up."

- "Everyone else has their life together."

- "What if I'm not good enough?"

But here's the truth: A thought is not a fact.

Thoughts are shaped by stress, trauma, and

childhood experiences. They are influenced by exhaustion, insecurity, other people's expectations, and past seasons you've outgrown. Not everything your brain says deserves your belief.

Reflection

When something triggers you, do you mostly feel fear, anger, shame, or numbness?

Curiosity Over Criticism

The quickest way to calm a spiraling mind is to focus it with a question.

Instead of:

♦ "What's wrong with me?"

Try asking:

♦ "What is this thought protecting me from?"

♦ "What am I feeling?"

♦ "What am I trying to avoid?"

In addition to this, ask:

♦ Is this anxiety or intuition?

♦ Is this fear or fact?

♦ What triggered this feeling?

♦ What do I need in this moment: rest, reassurance, truth, prayer?

Get clear about what you're feeling, then state it out loud. Curiosity turns panic into insight. Grace doesn't skip over the undeserving; it reaches everyone.

Ask Better Questions

The quality of your questions matters. Overthinking asks powerless questions like:

♦ "What if something goes wrong?"

♦ "What if I embarrass myself?"

♦ "What if I can't handle it?"

Understanding asks powerful questions, ones that empower, such as:

♦ "What if things turn out better than expected?"

♦ "What is the most realistic outcome?"

♦ "What am I capable of in this situation?"

♦ "What evidence do I have for this fear?"

Fear imagines catastrophe. Wisdom imagines possibility.

Facts vs. Feelings

Feelings matter; they are messengers. But they are not always accurate narrators. Practice separating what you know is true from what you're afraid is true. Here are some examples:

- **Feeling:** "I'm anxious."

- **Fact:** "I survived today and did my best."

- **Feeling:** "Nobody cares."

- **Fact:** "My mind is lonely, not my life."

Naming the difference keeps emotions from becoming reality.

Build Self-Trust

Overthinking thrives where self-trust is weak. Self-trust means:

- Believing you can handle what comes

- Knowing mistakes don't define you

- Accepting that you don't need every answer

- Recognizing your worth is not up for debate

You don't need a guaranteed outcome to move forward. You just need trust in yourself and trust in God.

Let Things Be

Not every situation needs a conclusion. Not every conversation needs closure. Not every emotion needs solving. Not everything needs a reaction. Some people mistake your patience for permission to walk all over you. Your good qualities are gifts to give to those who value them.

Peace often comes when you stop forcing clarity, accept uncertainty, and allow time to reveal what effort cannot. Letting things be is a spiritual practice. It means surrendering the control we were never meant to hold. Teaching your body that it is safe now, growing now, and that you are free now is part of peace.

Shortening the Spiral

Overthinking may still show up. We're human, after all. But the spiral shortens the more you slow down, interrupt the thought loops, and choose helpful actions. Other ways to shorten the spiral are to speak grace to yourself and turn anxiety into prayer.

Focus on what you can influence, and release what isn't yours to carry. Through practice and intention, your brain becomes a partner instead of a problem. And remember, you were never meant to earn your worth. You were born with it. By knowing your worth, you return to who you've always been.

Whole. Enough. Love. Chosen.

Water What You Want to Grow

Your mind is like a garden. You can't stop weeds from sprouting, but you can choose what grows strong. Water and nurture what you want to grow.

Water:

◆ Truth over assumption

◆ Grace over criticism

- ◆ Presence over fear

- ◆ Prayer over panic

- ◆ Curiosity over judgment

Over time, your thoughts reflect peace instead of chaos. Overthinking is not your destiny; understanding is.

When you learn to guide your mind gently, you stop battling yourself and start leading your own life with grace. You are the one who chooses what takes root. Replace overthinking with understanding, confusion with clarity, and chaos with compassion.

Every gentle thought you choose brings you closer to peace.

> *"Trust in the Lord with all your heart and lean not on your own understanding."*
>
> Proverbs 3:5–6 (NIV)

Faith quiets the mental spiraling by reminding us that we don't carry life alone.

Training Your Brain to Let Go

Many women carry the invisible weight of conversations, moments, and memories long after they've passed. We replay things we said, things we wish we had said, tones we could have softened, reactions we fear were misunderstood, or tiny embarrassing moments no one else remembers.

Our brains loop them like a movie stuck on repeat—all because we want to feel safe, prepared, understood, and in control. Women are wired to nurture, anticipate, and care, emotionally and relationally. For many of us, that means we analyze tone and facial expressions. We try to interpret silence and read between the lines. We question whether we disappointed someone and worry we offended or embarrassed ourselves.

We overthink not because we're weak but because we care deeply. But caring too much about what is already over can become a quiet form of self-torture.

Replaying events is the brain's attempt to prevent future pain, find closure that wasn't given, and solve problems that may not exist, rewrite reality into a safer ending, and ultimately avoid rejection or regret.

But no amount of rumination changes the past. In fact, overthinking often creates chaos that the situation itself never caused. This means that an uncomfortable five-second interaction can balloon into hours of self-criticism, shame spirals, and imaginary arguments, leaving you emotionally exhausted.

Most of the time, the other person isn't thinking about it at all. But we stay stuck because the brain mistakes rumination for responsibility, especially for women.

Women are conditioned from childhood to be "good girls"—to avoid conflict, smooth tension, and take responsibility for harmony. So when something feels off, unresolved, or awkward, our brain tries to fix it—internally—over and over.

This can lead to shame spirals, anxiety spikes, deep regret, and other uncomfortable emotions. We lose peace over imagined criticism. And the most painful part? Most of the stories we spin are not even true. We fill in the blanks with insecurity instead of facts.

The good news is that you can train your brain to let go, but it takes intention. This is where the practice of parsing out feelings from facts is key. Identify what happened (facts) instead of what you fear happened (feelings). Feelings and facts are not the same.

When your mind starts replaying a scene, say aloud, **"Stop. Not today. I release this."** It may feel silly, but your brain responds to interruption. Instead of the worst-case version, practice a new default: **"They probably didn't notice."** Because ninety-nine percent of the time, they didn't.

Finding Closure Within

Sometimes closure never comes externally. Offer it to yourself by writing a new script: **"It happened. I learned. I'm moving forward."**

If you didn't do anything harmful, let time neutralize it. Unless you keep them alive with your thoughts, most awkward moments fade.

How would you comfort a dear friend who was experiencing pain or emotional discomfort? Speak to yourself that way. Say: "Of course you're thinking about it; you care. But it's done. It doesn't define you." Leave it in the past.

Overthinking lives in the past. Happiness lives in the now. To live in the present, incorporate grounding practices such as deep breathing, prayer, practicing gratitude, or making a physical shift (walking, stretching, and playing).

Replaying events is a habit, not a character flaw. It protected you once, but it doesn't serve you now. The more you practice releasing old moments, the more mental space you reclaim for peace, joy, creativity, clarity, and connection.

And the truth is this: You are not the worst thing you've said. You are not the awkward moment you relive. You are not your past conversations on repeat.

You are growing. You are learning. And you deserve to live forward, not backward.

PART III: REDEFINING YOUR LIFE

Chapter 7:

GRATITUDE: THE SHORTCUT TO PEACE

G ratitude is often overlooked because it seems too simple to matter. People hear the word and think of holiday dinners or forced lists of "three things I'm thankful for."

But gratitude is not a **cliché**. It is a spiritual reset, a mental reframe, and a doorway into peace. Gratitude does not deny what hurts; it reminds you of what helps you endure it.

Gratitude Is:	What Gratitude Is NOT:
♦ Noticing goodness	♦ It's not ignoring pain.
♦ Acknowledging its source (people, life, God, circumstances)	♦ It's not pretending everything is perfect.
♦ Feeling appreciation for it	♦ It's not toxic positivity.

You can feel grief and gratitude at the same time.

Why Gratitude Works

Your brain is wired for survival, not happiness. It constantly scans for what's wrong, what could go wrong, or what needs fixing. That's helpful for safety. But for peace, it's exhausting.

Fortunately, gratitude interrupts that pattern. What you think about most, you become. When you intentionally notice what is good—even if small—your brain shifts from stress to steadiness, from scarcity to sufficiency, from overwhelm to clarity, and from pressure to peace.

Gratitude is not a mood booster. It is a powerful perspective shifter which:

♦ Calms your nervous system

♦ Deepens your connections

♦ Strengthens your resilience

Small Joys Are Big Joys

Gratitude wears everyday clothes. It lives in:

- A warm coffee in your hands

- A quiet morning

- An unexpected laugh

- The food in your pantry

- A text from someone who loves you

- The simple miracle of waking up

Joy multiplies when we notice it.

Gratitude in Hard Seasons

Gratitude isn't denial. It doesn't pretend pain is pleasant or storms are sunny. Real gratitude says, "This is tough, and I am not alone." It says: "I don't like this, but I see grace showing up."

Gratitude lightens the load so it doesn't crush you.

Reflection:

Do you find it easier to feel gratitude in peaceful times, or is it hardest when life feels heavy?

When Comparison Steals Joy

Comparison kills joy faster than failure. When you compare, you stop seeing your blessings. You measure your journey with someone else's tools. You feel behind, and you always want more.

But gratitude shifts the story to this: "I'm grateful for what God is doing in me."

Reflection:

When you compare, is it mostly about appearance, success, relationships, or inner growth?

Daily Practice

Gratitude grows like a muscle. Start practicing gratitude today. Try writing blessings down, telling someone you appreciate them, noticing small beauty, and whispering thanks even for ordinary things—especially for ordinary things. Give a simple but heartfelt "thank you" each morning.

You don't force gratitude, you practice it.

What Gratitude Unlocks

Gratitude expands what you see. Problems shrink. Burdens soften. Blessings multiply. Through practicing gratitude, you become more present and less anxious, more grounded and less restless.

Gratitude builds trust in God's faithfulness.

A Gentle Reminder

You don't need a new life to feel blessed, just new eyes. With one thank you at a time, gratitude is the shortest path from chaos back to peace.

"Rejoice always, pray continually, give thanks in all circumstances."

1 Thessalonians 5:16–18 (NIV)

Gratitude is a spiritual discipline that keeps the heart aligned with God's goodness.

The Pursuit of More

Human desire is a powerful thing, and it rarely sits still. We are wired with a longing for progress, curiosity, and growth. At our core, we are made in the image of a God who is infinite, so part of us naturally reaches for more. But in a world of endless options, comparison culture, and constant advertising, that longing can twist into striving that never satisfies.

We want more because we believe more will finally be enough: more money, more beauty, more attention, more success, more comfort, and more convenience. But "more" becomes a moving target. The moment we reach the next milestone, the finish line slides forward again.

Society fuels our cravings like oxygen to flame, with billions of dollars spent trying to convince us we need bigger homes, faster cars, and newer phones. More, more, more. Bigger, better, best. Lifestyles burgeon, and there are always the next upgrades and the latest experiences to pursue.

We are told that contentment equals complacency, that stillness is failure. We mistake having more for being more. But consuming never fills the ache;

it only stretches it wider. And at the root of the pursuit for more is a quiet fear: fear of not being enough, of being left behind, of missing out, of being unworthy or forgotten.

So we grasp, climb, buy, fix, upgrade, and accumulate—not just for pleasure, but for identity.

We believe the next achievement or purchase will heal old wounds, silence insecurity, prove our value, win approval, and validate our existence.

But here's the thing: The deepest reason we want more is spiritual. Ecclesiastes says God placed eternity in our hearts.

We are created with a longing that nothing earthly can satisfy. We chase more things because our spirits ache for more God. What we truly yearn for is more meaning, purpose, belonging, connection, peace, identity, fulfillment, and love.

We reach outward because we haven't looked inward or upward. The soul was created to desire, but it was also created to be satisfied by something eternal. But remember: Desire is not the problem, but unexamined desire is.

A holy hunger says: **"I want to grow, deepen, heal, and live aligned with God's calling."**

A worldly hunger says, **"I am never enough until I have more."**

One leads to peace. The other leads to exhaustion, comparison, and spiritual burnout.

We chase more until contentment dissolves, blessings grow invisible, gratitude dries up, and chaos becomes normal. You can't catch enough of anything to silence a soul that was made for heaven.

The shift happens when we learn that enough is a feeling, not a finish line, that fulfillment grows from gratitude, not accumulation, and that God gives abundance that doesn't require striving.

When desire is redirected toward meaning, purpose, and God-centered living, the ache for more becomes a path to joy rather than a treadmill of disappointment. Because the truth is simple, profound, and life-giving: We don't really want more things. We want more life.

More peace. More freedom. More presence. More purpose. More love. More of God. And those are things the world cannot sell us.

Chapter 8:

Stop Chasing Noise, Start Seeking Meaning

The world has never been louder, not just in sound, but in demands, distractions, expectations, alerts, opinions, and endless access to everyone else's lives. Noise isn't just what you hear. Noise is anything that pulls you away from who you are and what God has created you to do.

And if we don't learn to recognize the noise, we become ruled by it.

Check if the Noise Is Emotional, Not Just Mental

Often, **"overthinking"** is actually:

- Unprocessed fear

- Suppressed grief

- Old hurt resurfacing

- Chronic uncertainty

If your mind gets loud, especially when:

- You're alone

- It's night-time

- After certain interactions

There may be emotion asking to be felt.

Gentle self-question:

"What feeling is trying to speak through this noise?"

The Pull of Noise

Noise tells you to do more, be more, earn more, and impress more. It urges you not to fall behind. It shouts, "Hurry up, everybody's ahead of you!"

Noise feeds urgency. But meaning grows slowly. Without awareness, we live reactionary lives, where we are constantly responding and rarely receiving.

Noise fills your days but drains your spirit.

Sometimes the inner noise isn't fully **"internal."**

Quiet your environment by gently reducing:

- Constant news consumption

- Excess social media scrolling

- Too many opinions from others

- Multitasking overload

Reflection:

What am I mentally consuming all day? Your mind digests what you feed it.

How Noise Sneaks In

Noise is sneaky because it wears the costumes of normal life. It arrives as comparison, over-commitment, people-pleasing, and endless scrolling. It lingers as unwanted drama, saying yes automatically, and feeling guilty for wanting rest.

Noise convinces you that you have no choice. But you do—always.

Energy Leak map:

For 3 days, briefly note:

- What drained me today? (Be specific: conversation, scrolling, worry loop, etc.)

- What restored me today? (Even small things count)

- When did I feel most mentally noisy?

After a few days, patterns usually jump out.

Best if you:

- Feel constantly drained but don't know why.
- Notice many small leaks rather than one big problem.
- Want personalized insight before taking action.

7-Day Digital and Mental Detox

This is an action plan, not just awareness. The goal is to actively reduce overstimulation and give your nervous system breathing space.

It usually includes gentle steps like:

- Reducing screen input.
- Limiting mental clutter.
- Adding short quiet moments.
- Simplifying information intake.
- Creating tech boundaries.

Best if you:

- Already know you're overstimulated.
- Feel addicted to your phone or constant input.
- Want a structured reset plan.
- Feel mentally crowded most days.

Meaning Has a Different Pace

Meaning isn't loud, demanding, or flashy. It is quiet. Steady. Patient. Sacred.

Meaning is found in purpose, peace, and values. It exists in connection, contribution, and God's guidance.

A meaningful thought is:

♦ Calm in tone

♦ Useful or action-guiding

♦ Grounded in reality

♦ Repeats with quiet consistency

♦ Leaves you clearer (even if uncomfortable)

Meaningful thoughts move your life forward.

What is Mental Noise?

Mental noise is:

♦ Repetitive but unproductive

♦ Emotionally charged (panic, guilt, fear spiral)

♦ Hypothetical "what if" loops

♦ Urgent but not actually important

♦ Leaves you more confused or drained

♦ Noise keeps you stuck, not moving.

The 5-Second Filter

When a thought appears, gently ask:

- Is this actionable?
  - Yes → likely meaningful
  - No → likely noise

Living from the Inside Out

Most people live from the outside in, shaped by pressure, culture, expectations, and comparison. But meaning-rich living flips the equation, inviting you to live from the inside out.

Instead of asking:

- "What does everyone think I should do?"

You ask:

- "What does God want for my life?"

Instead of chasing approval, you honor alignment. Instead of reacting, you choose intentionally.

Your inner life, not the crowd, becomes the compass.

How to Recognize What Matters

Meaningful living comes from clarity. Ask yourself:

- What lights me up instead of wears me out?

- What do I want my life to feel like?

- ◆ Who am I trying to please: people or God?

- ◆ What values do I refuse to compromise?

- ◆ What do I want to be remembered for?

You may discover that what truly matters is simpler, slower, smaller, and more profound than you imagined.

The Fear of Missing Out

Noise thrives on **FOMO: the fear of missing out**. But here's the truth: Every yes is also a no.

Saying yes to noise often means saying no to rest, prayer, joy, creativity, family, presence, and purpose.

But meaning flips this: When you choose what matters, you stop missing your own life.

Practical boundaries that work:

- ◆ Don't start your morning with scrolling

- ◆ Unfollow accounts that trigger comparison

- ◆ Create social media "windows" instead of constant checking

- ◆ Take one low-stimulation day weekly

- ◆ You don't have to quit — just reduce the emotional exposure.

Who You Become in the Quiet

Silence is where meaning grows. Stillness is where clarity arrives. When you get quiet with God, you begin to hear your true thoughts and needs. You begin to see what is no longer aligned and where He is gently leading you. You begin to understand who you are meant to become.

Noise blocks identity. Quiet reveals it.

The Courage to Choose Less

Choosing meaning often begins with subtraction, not addition. You may need to release a commitment that drains you, a role you've outgrown, a friendship that no longer respects your boundaries, a habit that steals time and attention, or a dream that no longer reflects your heart.

Less noise equals more clarity. More clarity equals more purpose.

The Gentle Truth Most People Avoid

Every meaningful life requires brave exclusion. People who live peacefully are not doing everything. They are quietly, repeatedly choosing:

"This matters. That doesn't — for me."

Meaningful Living Changes You

A life led by meaning feels different. When your life has meaning, you:

- Wake up with direction instead of dread

- Feel more grounded than reactive

- Choose what aligns instead of what impresses

- Say no without guilt and say yes with joy

- Experience peace instead of pressure

- Value depth more than display

You stop living on autopilot. You start living on purpose.

Happiness Begins with Depth

Chasing noise is exhausting and deeply unsatisfying. Meaning **nourishes**. Meaning **steadies**. Meaning **lasts**.

You don't need the biggest, loudest life. You just need a life that's true to you. A life shaped with intention becomes a life shaped by joy. Meaning allows happiness to grow roots anchored in purpose.

A Gentle Invitation

Step away. Log off. Slow down. Turn inward. Ask God where your life needs focus. Follow the whisper, not the roar.

Noise wants your attention; meaning wants your heart. And once you choose depth over distraction, you stop chasing happiness. You begin living it.

> *"Seek first the kingdom of God and his righteousness, and all these things will be given to you as well."*
>
> Matthew 6:33 (NIV)

Meaning begins where worldly noise ends in seeking God first.

The News Distracts and Divides

The modern news cycle is no longer simply about informing us. It is about capturing us: our attention, our emotion, our outrage, and ultimately, our loyalty. Media outlets have learned something powerful, and that is that anger keeps us watching longer than joy ever will.

Instead of calmly reporting events, news channels frame stories to spark reaction, not reflection. They use loaded language, dramatic headlines, and exaggerated narratives to keep viewers glued to the screen. What used to be journalism has become entertainment—and the price is our unity.

We now live in a divisive world where red hates blue, blue hates red, and us versus them is the default mindset. But this division isn't accidental; it's by design. When we're divided, we stay engaged, emotional, defensive, and desperate for "our side" to win. And those in power profit from the fight.

Every click, every repost, every angry comment is currency. News creators understand that the brain responds faster to fear, outrage, and alarm than to nuance or calm. So the headlines shout:

- ♦ "CRISIS!"

- ♦ "BREAKING!"

- ♦ "DANGER!"

- ♦ "OUTRAGE!"

- ♦ "THEY are destroying everything!"

We are spoon-fed panic, blame, and half-truths. Facts are filtered, stories are slanted, and the most extreme voices are amplified because drama sells better than balance.

Over time, people stop seeing neighbors and start seeing threats, idiots, or enemies. Instead of being informed, we become indoctrinated into conflict.

Consuming too much news doesn't just inform our brains; it changes our nervous systems. It leads to anxiety, cynicism, chronic stress, distrust, anger, judgment, and emotional exhaustion. It perpetuates the perspective that the world is burning.

When you feel outraged or terrified every day, joy becomes a luxury your mind no longer believes it deserves. And the saddest part? Most people don't realize how much emotional space media occupies—space that could hold love, gratitude, creativity, connection, and peace.

The solution isn't ignorance. It's intentional consumption. Learn to protect your joy: Turn off the news except for specific check-in moments, read brief summaries instead of watching emotional commentary, step away from pointless political arguments, and limit social media scrolling. Spend more time living your life than analyzing headlines and intentionally replace outrage with prayer, community, and action that matters.

Ask yourself, **"Does this make me wiser or just more anxious?"** You are not obligated to absorb every crisis on Earth. You are not responsible for carrying the weight of every headline. You do not owe every media outlet your attention. Your peace is more valuable than their ratings.

A Balanced Goal

Aim to become:

- Informed but not flooded
- Aware but not overwhelmed
- Engaged but emotionally regulated

Seeking Unity

People on the opposite side of the political aisle are not villains. They are simply human beings shaped by different experiences, environments, fears, and values. If we turned off the news and spent time with real people face-to-face, we'd find more compassion and common ground. We'd remember that we're more similar than different. And we'd see humanity instead of headlines.

Division thrives in the noise. Unity grows in silence, conversation, and presence.

Turning off the news isn't giving up; it's coming home to yourself. When you unplug, your stress levels drop, your spirit softens, and your hope rises. Your perspective widens, your heart opens again, and you find that your life expands beyond conflict.

Chaos doesn't get to decide your mood. Anger doesn't have to be your default setting. Fear doesn't deserve to narrate your story.

When you limit the noise, you create space for peace, joy, beauty, and faith. You cultivate purpose, build meaningful relationships, and discover your truth. And that is where happiness lives.

Ask yourself:

- When have I understood someone better after meeting them?

- When have I misjudged tone over text?

- Whose presence makes me feel calmer without many words?

Your own experience will confirm this truth.

Chapter 9:

Boundaries: Your Secret Shield

Most of us weren't taught how to create healthy boundaries. We were taught to be accommodating, agreeable, helpful, and available—sometimes at the expense of ourselves.

But a life without boundaries is a life lived at the mercy of everyone else's wants, moods, and demands. Boundaries aren't walls that shut people out; they are doors that decide what's allowed in. It's the access you allow to others.

What Boundaries Really Are

Boundaries are the limits you set to protect your peace, time, and energy. They help you maintain your mental wellness, emotional health, and your God-given purpose.

Boundaries signal where you end and someone else begins. They help you stay responsible for yourself, not responsible for everyone else's reactions, emotions, or decisions.

Why Boundaries Feel Hard

If boundaries are healthy and necessary, why do they feel so uncomfortable?

Boundaries can be challenging to set and maintain because they require honesty, self- awareness, and releasing control. Setting boundaries means saying no and letting others feel how they feel, even if that means you risk disappointing someone.

For people who have spent years surviving by being **"easy," "dependable," "the fixer,"** or **"the strong one,"** boundaries can feel like betrayal. But betraying yourself to keep others comfortable is the real betrayal.

Signs You Need Boundaries

You may need stronger boundaries if you:

- Feel drained by certain people

- Say yes when your body is screaming no

- Consistently do more than your share

- Carry guilt for resting

- Avoid conflict to keep the peace

- Take responsibility for others' feelings

- Feel resentful even toward people you love

- Are exhausted but can't figure out why

- Refuse to quit something because it's not done

Your exhaustion is often a boundary issue, not a time issue.

A simple 3-step boundary practice

Step 1: Notice the drain
- Ask: What leaves me tense, heavy, or resentful?

Step 2: Name the limit (privately first)
- Example: I can't take late-night calls anymore.

Step 3: Communicate calmly and briefly
Use the formula:

"I'm not able to _ _ _ _ _ _ _ _, but I can _ _ _ _ _ _ _ _."

- Example: "I'm not able to respond immediately during the day, but I will reply in the evening."

Permission to Say No

"No" is not rejection. "No" is not disrespectful. "No" is not selfish. "No" is a complete sentence.

No is a tool—a tool God gives you to protect the life He entrusted you with.

Every time you say yes to something that drains you, you're unintentionally saying no to your rest, health, sanity, and purpose. Your yes becomes meaningful only when it is used selectively and intentionally.

A grounding reflection

Ask yourself tonight:

- Where did I abandon myself today?

- Where did I honor my limits?

- What is one small boundary I can practice tomorrow?

Expect Pushback

Not everyone will celebrate your boundaries. In fact, once you start erecting boundaries, it's likely that people will guilt-trip you, question you, or accuse you of changing or acting selfishly. Some may even withdraw when you stop over-giving.

Their reaction reveals their relationship to your lack of boundaries—not your worthiness to have them. Healthy people adjust. Unhealthy people resist. Let their response teach you what you need to know.

The truth is that boundaries don't work because others respect them. They work because you enforce them.

3 Questions to Reflect On

- ◆ Am I afraid of losing them if I stay firm?
- ◆ Do I feel guilty for protecting myself?
- ◆ What am I teaching them about how to treat me?

Types of Boundaries

You can set boundaries in every area of your life:

- ◆ **Emotional Boundaries:** "I can't carry this for you. I care, but I can't fix it."

- ◆ **Time Boundaries:** "I'm not available then."

- ◆ **Energy Boundaries:** "I don't have the capacity for this right now."

- ◆ **Communication Boundaries:** "I won't be spoken to that way."

- ◆ **Digital Boundaries:** "I check messages when I can, not instantly."

- ◆ **Relational Boundaries:** "If this becomes disrespectful, I will step away."

Boundaries don't complicate relationships—they clarify them.

Boundaries Protect Peace

Imagine your peace like a flame. Without boundaries, every gust—chaos, guilt, urgency, drama— blows out the flame.

But with boundaries, your flame becomes sheltered, protected, steady, and strong.

Boundaries are the difference between living resentfully and living joyfully, between reacting to life and creating it. They are not optional. They are spiritual self-care.

You Teach People How to Treat You

By what you accept, tolerate, or participate in, you teach others how to treat you. When you speak up kindly, set clear limits, enforce your no, and honor your needs, you are saying to others: **"I am worthy of love and respect."**

Boundaries are not about controlling others; they are about honoring yourself.

The Freedom on the Other Side

At first, boundaries feel like taking things away. But eventually, you realize that boundaries have much to offer you, including time, energy, mental clarity, and self-respect. Boundaries can help you realize healthier relationships, and more calmness, peace, and intentional joy.

By setting and maintaining boundaries, you stop living on everyone else's timeline and start living on your own God-led path. Boundaries don't separate you from people; they separate you from chaos.

A New Way Forward

Boundaries are not a one-time act. They are a practice. You will set them imperfectly. You will forget sometimes. You will slip back into old habits.

But you will get better with repetition. And every time you choose your well-being, your heart grows stronger.

Remember, you cannot pour from an empty cup. You cannot heal someone while you bleed. You cannot change another person. You cannot carry every load and walk freely.

Boundaries are not selfish; they are your secret shield. Protect your peace with intention. Honor your capacity with courage. Walk in the dignity of your God-given worth.

> *"Above all else, guard your heart, for everything you do flows from it."*
>
> Proverbs 4:23 (NIV)

Boundaries are biblical. Guarding your heart protects your life.

Boundary journaling prompt

Write for 5 minutes:

- ◆ Who drains me the most lately?
- ◆ What do I keep tolerating that hurts me?

- ✦ What boundary am I avoiding because it feels uncomfortable?

Clarity reduces emotional confusion.

The Invisible Standard

Every woman carries an invisible standard—a boundary line that tells the world what she will accept and allow. Sometimes we set that standard with our words.

But more often, we set it with our tolerance, our silence, and our willingness to absorb discomfort so someone else can stay comfortable.

Many women have been conditioned to be agreeable, stay polite, and keep the peace. We're raised to avoid hurting feelings or rocking the boat, and to put others first, no matter what.

So instead of saying, "That hurt" or "I need support," we swallow the sting and smile through it. And without realizing it, we train the people around us that our needs are optional. The truth is simple and powerful: Whatever we tolerate, we teach. When we accept disrespect, inconsistency, or neglect—even quietly—we normalize being treated that way because we're afraid to risk conflict, disappointment, or rejection.

People often don't change behavior that benefits them. If someone gives the bare minimum and still gets access to your time, your energy, or your heart, they'll keep giving the bare minimum. This doesn't mean women cause mistreatment—never. But patterns persist when they are unchallenged. Sometimes worth is tied to being the "good one," which is conditional love, usually started in childhood. She is expected to perform, behave, hold it together, and always do the right thing. She's not allowed to be weak, which leads to emotional numbness and anxiety. So she doesn't learn to feel emotions, only how to suppress them.

Tolerating crumbs doesn't make someone step up; it teaches them they never needed to bring the whole loaf. Healthy relationships require honesty, communication, mutual respect, and emotional reciprocity. Boundaries must be honored. And boundaries don't push people away; they reveal those who are willing to meet you where you are.

There are powerful, respectful ways to shift the dynamic without drama or hostility. Awareness is the first step. Practice saying:

- "This doesn't feel fair."

- "I'm giving more than I'm receiving."

- "My feelings are being overlooked."

You don't need a speech—just truth. Here are some more options to try:

- "That didn't feel good to me."

- "I'm not available to do that this time."

- "I need follow-through if we're going to continue this."

- "I deserve respect when we talk."

Short, steady sentences carry power.

Sometimes, though, words won't teach. That's when you need to express your boundaries in other ways. For example, you can stop explaining, apologizing, and jumping at every request. Return messages on your timeline. Step back from one- sided relationships. People notice the shift.

Boundary-setting only works if it lasts longer than the guilt or anxiety that follows. You may feel uncomfortable. That's normal. Growth always does.

If someone gets upset because you stop allowing mistreatment, that tells you who they are. Healthy people adjust. Unhealthy people protest. Either way, you gain clarity.

Teaching people how to treat you isn't about toughness; it's about integrity, dignity, and emotional stewardship. You deserve relationships where effort is mutual, your feelings and needs are valued, and your presence is appreciated, not assumed.

Knowing your worth is not arrogance, ego, or entitlement. It is clarity. Clarity about who you are, what you deserve, and how God created you to live. It is remembering that your value was assigned by heaven, not negotiated with people.

How Women Are Taught to Measure Their Worth

Most women were taught early to measure their worth by how useful, helpful, and agreeable they are. Their worth is measured by how much they sacrifice, how little they need, and how well they absorb discomfort so others don't have to. Because crying, fear, and mistakes were not allowed.

We grow up believing:

♦ "If I give enough, maybe I'll be loved."

♦ "If I'm perfect enough, maybe I'll be chosen."

♦ "If I don't ask for anything, maybe I'll be kept."

But a woman who believes she must earn her worth never gets to rest—because worth based on performance always demands more. Your worth does not come from your body, productivity, role, relationships, success, sacrifices, or the opinions of others.

Your worth came from the Hand that shaped you. You are worthy because God breathed life into you. You are made in His image. You are chosen, wanted, and known. You are loved before you lift a finger. You carry a divine purpose no one else can fulfill.

You cannot be "more" worthy, and you cannot be "less" worthy. Worth is fixed, eternal, and unshakable.

Every time you over explain yourself, apologize for existing, accept crumbs instead of nourishment, tolerate disrespect, shrink so others feel comfortable, or silence your needs—it isn't because you're weak. It's because somewhere along the way, you forgot who you are.

The world, trauma, rejection, and exhaustion have a way of slowly convincing a woman she is disposable, replaceable, or lucky to be chosen at all. But you are not lucky—you are valuable. And valuable things are not handled carelessly.

When you know your worth, you stop chasing people who don't show up and begging for unreciprocated love. You stop negotiating with disrespect. You stop over- functioning in relationships. You stop auditioning for a seat at tables God never intended you to sit at. You stop clinging to crumbs and start expecting whole meals.

A woman anchored in worth is calm, clear, and easy to love because she loves herself. She is hard to guilt, manipulate, or control.

Worth is magnetic. It draws the right people toward you and repels the wrong ones without you saying a word. You don't have to declare your worth loudly. Quietly knowing your worth changes how you speak and show up.

You begin to live as someone who believes deeply that:

◆ "Good things are not too much to ask for."

◆ "Respect is required."

◆ "My feelings matter."

◆ "My voice matters."

Remembering Your Worth

You are not learning your worth—you are remembering it. You are peeling away old lies and false beliefs. You are rewriting generational scripts, trauma messages, and cultural conditioning. Worth isn't something you become. It is something you awaken to. And once you see it, you cannot unsee it.

You stop showing up as a beggar and start showing up as a beloved daughter of God, one who knows her value because He declared it first.

One of the greatest lies women battle is the belief that their value rises and falls based on what they do. But identity is not earned but bestowed. The moment you took your first breath, heaven declared something over you that the world could never take away: that you are a daughter of the King. Not a servant scrambling for approval. Not a stranger hoping to be accepted. Not a mistake or an afterthought. You are a chosen daughter with royal inheritance running through your soul.

God says:

♦ You are loved.

♦ You are treasured.

♦ You are seen.

♦ You are known.

♦ You are chosen.

- ◆ You are redeemed.

- ◆ You are enough.

- ◆ You are mine.

He reminds you that you are not your circumstances. You are not your scars. You are not your insecurity or your past. You are what God says you are, and He never changes His mind.

When you know you belong to the King, you stop living like a pauper. Instead, a daughter of royalty is different in the way she walks, loves, speaks, and carries herself. With quiet confidence, she expects—and receives—dignity and respect.

She doesn't beg for love from people when she already has love from God. She doesn't chase validation. She doesn't shrink to make others comfortable. She knows she was created to shine.

Royalty is not arrogance. It is alignment with who God says you are.

You are valuable because God says you are.

If a painting becomes valuable because of the artist, how priceless must you be, crafted by the hands that shaped galaxies? God doesn't make disposable people. He creates masterpieces with eternal purpose. You are valuable because of your position in the family of God. You are adopted into the kingdom, sealed with promise, filled with purpose. You are set apart with destiny and called with intention. You are held with love that cannot be earned or lost.

There is no label the world can stamp on you that outweighs the one God already wrote on your soul: beloved.

Too many women live as if the world is the authority on their worth. But the world didn't create you. You are not too much: too emotional, too loud, too complicated, too broken, too old, and too late.

Those aren't God's words. Those are wounds talking, including cultural wounds. Instead, God calls you His handiwork, His daughter. You are a light-bearer, an image-bearer. You are a Kingdom carrier and overcomer. Above all, you are more than enough.

And nothing the world speaks over you can erase what God designed within you. This world may try to shrink you, shame you, or redefine you, but heaven has already crowned you with identity, authority, and purpose.

The invitation now is to live like it. This means choosing to walk away from disrespect, to release what was never yours to carry, to ask boldly, and to set boundaries with confidence. It means to love fully, to choose peace over chaos, and to believe what God says even when you don't feel it. It means to stand tall as someone deeply loved.

You are not begging at the edges of God's table— you are seated at it. A daughter does not beg. A daughter belongs. A daughter inherits. A daughter reigns with humility and power.

You are royalty—and the world will try to make you forget. But every morning you wake up breathing, heaven whispers again:

- ◆ "You are who I say you are."

- ◆ "You are mine."

- ◆ "You are loved without condition."

- ◆ "Walk like a daughter of the King."

Chapter 10:

PROTECTING YOUR PEACE

Your peace is the invisible fuel behind every part of your life: your thoughts, your mood, your relationships, your dreams, your decisions, your faith, and your ability to show up for the things that matter. It is your most precious resource.

Yet most of us guard everything except our peace. We lock our doors at night. We protect our money. We secure our phones with passwords. We track packages from the moment they ship. But we let people, pressures, distractions, and demands drain our energy without thinking twice.

Protecting your peace is not selfish. It is essential. Inner peace leaks through constant stimulation.

Peace filters to apply:

- Less unnecessary news
- Less comparison scrolling
- Less exposure to negative conversation
- More silence between activities

Inner peace does not mean:

- No stress
- No difficult people
- No hard days

It means:

- You return to yourself faster
- You don't stay disturbed for long
- You respond instead of react

Peace Speaks Before Words

Peace is the first thing people notice about you. You can feel when someone is warm or cold, calm or chaotic. You can sense when someone is safe or draining, present or distracted, and uplifted or depleted.

The way you carry yourself shapes the atmosphere around you. You can walk into a room with peace and shift the entire tone, or you can arrive exhausted and feel yourself crumble inside it.

Where Peace Goes

Your energy is being spent constantly, whether you're aware of it or not. Your energy flows toward work, family, relationships, and responsibilities, among many other things.

But energy leaks through misaligned commitments, unresolved emotions, and people-pleasing. It can be drained by overthinking, overburdening yourself with other people's problems, and spending too much time on devices. Chaos quietly drains you until you realize you're running on fumes.

Inner peace is not fragile — but it is sensitive to daily habits. Most people don't lose peace because life is too hard. Inner peace doesn't leave you. It gets crowded out.

♦ Too much enters your mind- noise, opinions, expectations, and other people's chaos.

♦ Too many yeses pull you away from yourself-until you feel scattered, stretched and quietly disconnected.

♦ Too little stillness keeps you running-until your own voice gets drowned out.

Inner peace is not something you find. It's something you protect.

You protect it by choosing what gets access to your mind.

Peace Givers vs. Peace Drainers

One of the most transformational acts of self-awareness is identifying what fills you and what empties you.

Peace Givers include:

- Deep breaths

- Prayer or meditation

- Sleep and rest

- Time in nature

- Creative expression

- Healthy relationships

- Laughter

- Grounding

- Worship

- A walk outside

- Reading something uplifting

Peace Drainers include:

- Overcommitting

- Constant comparison

- Internal criticism

- Toxic relationships

- Endless scrolling

- Rushing all day

- Saying yes when you mean no

- Conflict without resolution

- Trying to fix everyone

- Ignoring your needs

Protecting your peace starts with noticing and then choosing wisely.

Your Peace Is Sacred

Somewhere in life, we absorbed the idea that "good" people give until they're empty. But no one benefits from your burnout. You are not called to be everyone's answer.

You are called to remain grounded enough to follow God's leading. Your peace is a gift, not a resource for the world to drain.

Relationships and Peace

Every relationship either nourishes or depletes you. Ask yourself: Who leaves me feeling lighter and who leaves me feeling heavier? Who respects my boundaries and who crosses them? Who cheers when I rest? Who feels threatened when I grow? Who makes me try too hard?

Your relationships send you clues. Some people are wells—you draw life from them. Others are drains—you pour out more than you receive. You don't have to cut everyone off. But you do get to choose your access points.

You can invite peace into a relationship, but you cannot force it alone.

Healthy peace requires:

♦ Willingness on both sides

♦ Emotional responsibility

♦ Mutual respect

If only one person is doing all the emotional work, the relationship may feel calm on the surface but heavy underneath.

Emotional Labor Costs Peace

You can love people deeply without carrying their emotional baggage. Say to yourself: "I care about you, but your healing is not my job."

Their healing is their responsibility. This frees you from becoming the fixer, absorbing others' stress, feeling guilty for not solving problems, being the world's emotional first responder, and over-functioning to the point of resentment.

Compassion has boundaries. Empathy has limits. Your heart is not a landfill. You are not an emotional dumping ground.

Quick Self-Check (You Can Answer Now)

Rate each from 0–5:

Condition	Rating
I replay upsetting situations in my mind.	
Small things trigger strong reactions	
My body often feels tense or on edge.	
It takes me a long time to emotionally recover.	
My mood spills onto others.	

If several are 3 or above, your emotions may currently be costing your peace — but the good news is this is very workable and reversible.

Rest Is Required

Rest is not a luxury. It is survival. Rest is profound in that it restores:

♦ Clarity

♦ Joy

♦ Perspective

♦ Creativity

♦ Emotional balance

- Physical health

- A sense of possibility

- Connection with God

Busyness whispers, "You don't have time to rest." Wisdom responds, "You don't have time not to." Rest is the spiritual act of trusting God enough to stop.

So, begin to prioritize rest and protect your peace. This can take many forms, including:

- Saying no without guilt

- Taking breaks without apology

- Choosing slowness

- Ending conversations when they turn toxic

- Limiting access to draining people

- Unplugging from screens

- Going home early

- Doing nothing on purpose

- Ending your day before you're empty

- Creating space for God to refill you

Your peace is your life force. Guard it like the precious resource it is.

The Ripple Effect

The more you protect your peace:

- The better decisions you make

- The more patient you become

- The stronger your boundaries grow

- The deeper your joy feels

- The more grateful you become

- The brighter your presence shines

- The more available you are for what truly matters

- The more you have to give

You no longer react to life. You respond with intention.

A New Way of Being

Protecting your peace is not about being unavailable or disconnected. It's about valuing and prioritizing your happiness. It is about showing up with purpose, not panic. Presence, not pressure. Clarity, not chaos. Joy, not resentment. God's strength, not your own depletion.

It is about honoring your limits so you can live aligned with your calling. When your peace is nourished, your happiness rises naturally, your faith has space to breathe, and your life begins to feel like your own again.

Protect your energy. Honor your capacity. Walk gently with yourself. Move slowly when needed. And let your life reflect what your soul was designed for: peace.

> *"Don't be dejected and sad, for the joy of the Lord is your strength!"*
>
> Nehemiah 8:10 (NLT)

Becoming Available to What Truly Matters

Most of us aren't missing joy because life is empty; we're missing it because our days are too full of things that don't matter. We move so fast, manage so much, say yes so often, and carry so many unnecessary responsibilities that the things meant to nourish our souls get squeezed into whatever time is left, which is usually none.

We want to slow down, be more intentional, and live with meaning, but life pulls us in a thousand directions: work, family, obligations, errands, notifications, expectations, noise, and invisible pressure to be productive in every moment. We end up spending energy on what's urgent rather than what's important. And in the process, we lose connection to the people, passions, and purpose that make life rich.

Being available to what matters doesn't start with adding new things. It starts with removing what drains you. To be available to the things that matter—your family, faith, health, joy, and your life's dreams—you must become unavailable to chaos, people- pleasing, and other energy drainers. You can't say yes to your purpose while saying yes to everything.

Busyness Makes Us Unavailable

Women, especially, are taught to stretch themselves thin, believing that exhaustion equals love or obligation equals loyalty. But busyness doesn't make us valuable; it makes us unavailable to loved ones, joyful hobbies, restorative rest, and the fulfilment of our faith. It makes us unavailable to the whispers of God that only come when we're quiet.

Life becomes meaningful not when we do more, but when we do the right things. Choosing what matters means letting go of what no longer serves you and creating boundaries without apology. It means leaving space on your calendar by declining invitations that drain you. Choosing what matters means practicing the power of no and simplifying your priorities to match your values.

This is not selfish; it is **stewardship.** The most precious moments in life rarely shout for your attention. They are beautiful in their subtlety and may include:

◆ An unplanned conversation with your child

◆ A walk that clears your mind

◆ A hobby that reconnects you with yourself

◆ Laughter around the dinner table

◆ A prayer whispered before sleep

◆ A slow cup of coffee at sunrise

- A weekend morning with no plans

- The stillness where God's voice gets louder

If your life is too crowded, these moments slip by unnoticed or don't have the space to occur at all. Making room for them is an act of honor to yourself, your family, and your Creator.

Becoming available to what matters is not a one-time decision. It's a lifestyle shift. Begin by determining who and what brings you peace and makes you feel alive. Consider what you want to remember about this season of life. Write down your answers and let them be your compass.

Next, take an audit of how you spend your time, attention, mental energy, and emotional labor. Consider if each activity is supporting the life you want or distracting you from it. Not everything deserves equal access to you. Remove what doesn't align, even if others don't understand.

Build margin, as margin makes room for rest, laughter, spontaneity, delight, and presence. When you build margin, you become more available to what matters. Life feels lighter. Anxiety quiets and creativity emerges. Relationships deepen, clarity returns. In short, your soul breathes again, and God has room to speak into your days.

You stop reacting to life and start experiencing it. Slowly, you realize that the life you want isn't somewhere out there, waiting until you have more time, money, freedom, or certainty. It's right here. Now. It's already happening. It just needs room to unfold.

Being available to what matters is how you shift from surviving your life to living it with joy, intention, and peace.

Putting Yourself First

Many women are raised to believe that being "good" means being selfless—not just in spirit, but to the point of emotional depletion. Women grow up believing care is love and exhaustion is normal. And many internalize a dangerous belief: "I'll take care of myself later." But later rarely comes.

Putting yourself last doesn't just drain your time; it drains your spirit. When women take responsibility for everyone else and ignore their own needs, their peace slowly dissolves. Stress becomes a constant hum. Resentment quietly builds. Emotional fatigue becomes normal. Personal goals fade. Joy and rest get swallowed by the needs of others.

When women spend all their energy keeping the home, workplace, friendships, or family afloat, they often have nothing left for themselves. Nobody can pour from an empty well, yet women keep dipping into dry riverbeds hoping something is left.

Here's the truth: Putting yourself last feels noble, but it is quietly destructive. Women put themselves last for many reasons. Most notably, they've been conditioned to hold everything together. They confuse self-care with selfishness, fear disappointing others, or don't want to burden anyone else. They associate rest with guilt and don't believe their needs carry equal weight. They may also be praised more for giving than receiving.

Many women don't even know what they need because they stopped asking themselves years ago. And beneath this lack of knowing oneself is a false but powerful belief: "Everyone else matters more than I do."

You Matter

Reclaiming peace is not selfish. It is essential, spiritual, and sometimes life-saving. Here's how to start remembering that you matter. Every day, say aloud to yourself: "I deserve care too." Permission must come from inside before boundaries can be set outside.

Ask yourself what you're feeling, carrying, and what you need right now. Is it rest, space, support? Something else? Awareness is power.

A Simple, Powerful "No"

Women often justify every no with a paragraph. Practice simple boundaries:

- ◆ "No, I can't."

- ◆ "No, that won't work for me."

- ◆ "No, I'm resting today."

No reasons required.

Saving everyone trains them to stay dependent, and trains you to stay exhausted. Let adults do adult things. You are not the emergency hotline for every crisis.

Making Time

Block time on your calendar for things that fill your cup: rest, joy, prayer, friendships, hobbies, exercise, and stillness. If you don't schedule you, no one will. Choosing yourself may feel wrong initially, as your nervous system is used to self-neglect. But stay the course. New habits always feel strange before they feel freeing.

You matter as much as the people you serve. Your needs count. Your peace is holy. Your well-being impacts everyone, especially those you love.

A woman who protects her peace flourishes. She becomes more:

♦ Grounded

♦ Loving

♦ Joyful

♦ Present

♦ Patient

Most importantly, she becomes more connected to herself and to God.

When you put yourself on the list—not last, but equal—you finally live like someone who believes their life is important. That their peace matters. That their soul deserves rest. And that isn't selfish; it's sacred stewardship of the one life God gave you.

The Discomfort of Putting Yourself First

For many women, putting themselves first feels uncomfortable, even wrong. We've been conditioned to equate selflessness with goodness and exhaustion with love. So the moment we prioritize our own needs, boundaries, or well-being, guilt shows up like an old, familiar shadow whispering, **"Who do you think you are?"**

But the truth is, God never called us to disappear under the weight of everyone else's expectations. He called us to steward our lives, and caring for ourselves is part of that calling. The first step to putting yourself first is rewriting the belief that you must earn rest, attention, or care. You don't have to justify your emotional, physical, or spiritual needs. They matter simply because you matter.

Every time you choose to meet your own needs—whether by saying no, taking a break, asking for help, or stepping away from chaos—you reclaim space in your life that was always meant for you. When guilt arises, notice it, name it, and then remind yourself gently that feeling bad does not mean you're doing something wrong. It means you're breaking a generational habit.

Putting yourself first is also an act of love—not just for you, but for the people around you. When you nourish your spirit, your patience expands. When you are rested, you show up calmer and clearer. When you set boundaries, you stop resenting the people you love. When you tend to your emotional needs, you become more whole, and a whole woman loves better than an empty one ever could.

Another essential part of shedding guilt is letting others take responsibility for their own lives. Women often carry burdens God never assigned them: other people's emotions, expectations, reactions, disappointments, crises, or chaos. When you stop absorbing everything and allow people to handle their own choices, you lighten your load and honor their growth.

Most importantly, putting yourself first aligns with God's design for balance and joy. Even Jesus—the most selfless human who's ever lived—rested, withdrew from crowds, slept on boats, and walked away to pray. If the Son of God didn't run on empty, neither should you.

Your worth isn't measured by how much you do or how many people you please. You are worthy because God says you are. Little by little, guilt fades as self-worth grows.

Putting yourself first becomes less about pushing others aside and more about finally standing where you belong: in your own life, in your own priorities, and in the center of God's care for you. When you choose yourself with love and intention, you teach the world, your family, and your own heart the truth you already deserve to believe: My needs matter. **My life matters**. And I am allowed to take up space.

PART IV: CENTERING FAITH

Chapter 11:

FILLED FROM WITHIN: FAITH, FULFILLMENT, AND THE PEACE GOD GIVES

There is a longing inside every human heart: a quiet ache, a gentle tug, a sense that something more exists beneath the surface of our lives. You can feel it in the middle of joy and in the center of struggle. You can feel it when life is full and when life feels empty. You feel it even on your best days. It's that whisper saying, **"You were made for more than this."**

We spend years, or decades, trying to fill that longing on our own. We try to replace that longing with:

- Accomplishments, achievements, and approval

- Relationships, praise, and possessions

- Productivity, busyness, and distractions

But when the noise fades, and the world gets quiet, we're reminded of a truth the soul never forgets: Nothing external will ever fully satisfy what only God can fill.

Clue:

- If you imagine quiet → you may be longing for peace.

- If you imagine being seen → you may be longing for validation or connection.

- If you imagine escape → you may be longing for freedom or rest.

- Irritated when ignored → longing to be valued

- Drained around people → longing for boundaries or solitude

- Jealous of others' freedom → longing for autonomy

- Envy of someone's calm → you long for inner peace

- Envy of someone's success → you long for growth or recognition

- Envy of close friendships → you long for deeper connection

- Socially drained → you may long for solitude or authentic connection

- Mentally overwhelmed → you may long for simplicity

- Emotionally numb → You may long for meaning or purpose Pause and scan your body when you feel restless:

- Tight chest → often unmet emotional needs

- Heavy shoulders → burden or responsibility overload

- Restless energy → suppressed desire for change

- Hollow feeling → lack of meaning or connection

The Hole Inside Us All

Every one of us carries a space inside that is uniquely shaped for God: for meaning, for spiritual connection, for love greater than human love, for peace deeper than logic, for hope beyond circumstance.

We try to pour life into that space, but life leaks. We try to earn happiness, but it slips through our fingers when storms come. We try to build a life so full that nothing could possibly feel missing, yet it feels incomplete anyway. Not because we are broken, but because we are wired for something eternal.

Long-term emptiness often comes from misalignment.

Ask yourself softly:

- Where in my life am I shrinking to fit?

- What feels heavy but I keep tolerating?

- What gives me even small moments of aliveness?

Faith Changes How You Live

Faith does not remove struggle. Faith transforms how you walk through it. With faith, you no longer chase everything to feel complete. You stop believing happiness is something you earn. You let go of the exhausting pressure to do life alone. You trust that you are held, even when life is uncertain. You stop striving to fill yourself with things that don't last.

Faith anchors your heart to something bigger than circumstance. It says: Even in lack, I am not empty. Even in waiting, I am not abandoned. Even in chaos, I am not alone. Even in loss, I am deeply loved.

Faith helps most when it is secure and compassionate.

It can become harmful if it turns into:

- Constant guilt and fear

- Fatalism ("nothing I do matters")

- Spiritual avoidance of real problems

- judgment toward self or others

    Healthy faith says:

- "Trust deeply and still take wise action."

Faith doesn't always make life easier. But for many people, it makes life steadier, more meaningful, and less lonely inside.

Contentment: When Enough Becomes Enough

Faith teaches a rare gift in a world of constant wanting: contentment. Contentment is the peace of knowing:

◆ I am blessed even here.

◆ I have enough for today.

◆ I don't need to compete, compare, or chase.

◆ I am protected, provided for, and safe.

Contentment does not mean you stop dreaming; it means you stop believing joy is on the other side of "more." Instead, you learn to see beauty right where your feet are planted.

A Gentle Night Reflection

Before sleep, write:

◆ One thing that was enough today

◆ One thing is still in progress

◆ One thing you are quietly grateful for

Over weeks, this rewires the emotional baseline toward contentment.

The Role of Surrender

One of the kindest parts of faith is surrender. Surrender reminds you that you don't have to carry every burden yourself, that you don't need to figure everything out, and that you can trust that God has a bigger plan for you.

When you surrender, the weight lifts, anxiety loosens, and the need for control softens. The future feels less frightening. Peace feels possible. You stop anxiously gripping life with both hands and let God hold what you were never meant to carry alone.

When You Let God Fill You

Something shifts when you let God take up residence in the space inside your soul. You become more gentle with yourself, more trusting of others, and more appreciative of the simple things. You feel less shaken by circumstances, less desperate for validation, and less swayed by chaos. Overall, you are more deeply anchored in who you are and who guides you.

Faith does not just comfort; it reorients you. It becomes the lens through which you see your life. Chaos may still knock at the door, but peace—God's peace—answers.

Faith and Happiness Walk Together

When your joy comes from God, it is steadier, deeper. It lasts longer. It isn't easily taken. It doesn't depend on the approval of others. It doesn't disappear when life gets messy.

Faith does not remove life's difficulties, but it changes your relationship with them. Happiness that depends only on circumstances rises and falls.

Happiness supported by faith tends to become:

♦ More stable

♦ More resilient

♦ More meaningful

Epilogue: The Journey Continues

There is a quiet moment that comes when you finish a book like this: a moment where you exhale, close the page, and return to your own life. But this time, you return differently. Not because everything outside has changed, but because something inside of you has.

You now carry:

♦ Awareness of your worth

♦ Permission to choose peace

♦ Confidence to protect yourself

♦ Broader faith

♦ Courage to release what no longer fits

♦ A clearer vision of what matters most

♦ A softer, steadier belief that happiness begins within you

♦ And a deeper connection to the God who meets you wherever you are

A New Beginning

What you've read is not a finish line; it's a doorway. You will still have busy days. You will still feel overwhelmed sometimes. You will still forget to rest and slip back into old patterns. That is what being human looks like.

But now you hold tools, truths, and language to help you come back home more quickly. You know how to:

- Pause

- Notice

- Ask better questions

- Protect your peace

- Listen to your own voice

- Step away from chaos

- Choose meaning over noise

- And find joy in the middle of real life

The Daily Journey

Happiness isn't a destination you reach and stay in. It is a practice, a rhythm, a returning. Every morning, you begin again with a gentle choice, a gratitude list, a whispered prayer:

- "Today, I choose peace."

- "Today, I choose joy."

- "Today, I choose myself."

Over time, these choices shape who you are becoming: someone rooted, rested, and ready.

You Are Not Doing This Alone

God walks every step with you. He steadies your heart. He fills the empty places. He reminds you of your value when you forget. He guides you back to peace when you drift toward chaos.

Even when life feels unsteady, God is not. And as you breathe deeper, listen closer, and surrender more often, you will notice that you were never walking it alone.

A Life You Don't Need to Escape From

More than anything, I hope this book helps you build a life that you don't want a vacation from—a life you do not need to run from, numb out to survive, or apologize for wanting. A life where:

♦ Rest is allowed

♦ Joy is accessible

♦ Boundaries are respected

♦ Gratitude comes easily

♦ Overthinking has less power

♦ Chaos is no longer in control

♦ Your world feels safe and steady

♦ Happiness is not chased, but cultivated

A Blessing for Your Next Chapter

May your days be slow enough to notice beauty......
May your heart grow bold enough to protect your peace.......
May your mind soften enough to trust what you cannot see........
May your relationships reflect the value you've placed on yourself........
May you wake grateful, live present, and rest deeply........
And may you feel God's presence not just in quiet moments, but in the messy, miraculous rhythms of everyday life.........

You are stepping forward into a new chapter, one written intentionally, lived authentically, and guided by the truth that joy was never lost. It simply needed space to rise. You are made for peace. You are worthy of happiness. And you are strong enough to choose it, over and over again. The journey continues—and you are ready.

www.ingramcontent.com/pod-product-compliance
Lightning Source LLC
Chambersburg PA
CBHW051237070726
47594CB00013B/353